The Alchemy of Art

"Birdhouse In Your Soul" Painting by Hirschten

The Alchemy of Art
Stories for the Classroom

ADDIE HIRSCHTEN

HOLLY
TREE PRESS

Holly Tree Press Publishing
Indianapolis, Indiana, USA
ISBN: 0-692-45892-1
ISBN-13: 978-0-692-45892-1

COVER ARTWORK AND DESIGN
Addie Hirschten- "Birdhouse In Your Soul" Painting
Red Raven Graphics http://redravendp.blogspot.pt/ - Cover Design

FIRST EDITION

DEDICATION

This book is dedicated to all who love creation,
and
to my fourth grade teacher, Mrs. Jane Luhn, who not only
told me that I should write a book but also introduced me to
Greek mythology.

CONTENTS

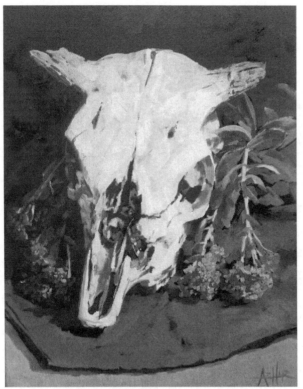

"Sedums and Skull" Painting by Hirschten

INTRODUCTION

The inspiration for this project came when I started teaching art classes for children through the outreach department of the Indianapolis Art Center.

I would start each lesson sharing a story from folklore or

an artist's biography. Sometimes the stories gave us pictures to depict when we created the daily art project. Other times the stories hit upon what it means to be an artist and why we create art. Over time I started incorporating the stories into the classes I teach for adults as well. This book was created from that research.

Each story focuses on a different type of artist. In this book you will find painters, sculptors, musicians and even chefs. What the artist creates is not the important element. Look for the process they go through to get to the finished product. How do the characters face conflict and resolve it? When you are reading these stories, look for ways to apply the message of the tale to your own life or those of your students.

The most difficult part of writing this book was making the connection between the visual arts and the written word. Art is a language that is used to express what we cannot say in words. This is why it can be challenging to write an artist's statement. Yet through the context of these folktales and true life stories the purpose of art unfolds. I found many of these tales comforting because they strengthened and helped to define my artistic convictions.

Whether you are an artist seeking inspiration or a teacher looking for materials to share, I hope this book helps you. I believe that every person can be an artist. Every person can harness the energy of creation, break down materials and form them into something new. This is the alchemy of art. Alchemy was the medieval science of transforming ordinary base metals into something of higher value such as gold. With art we take materials and manipulate them until we get something extraordinary.

I often say to my students, "You can do anything I can do. It will just come out with a different voice." May these stories guide you.

****

*"The root meaning of art is to fit together
and we all do this every day. Not all of us
are painters but we are all artists. Each
time we fit things together we are creating;
whether it is to make a loaf of bread,
a child, or a day."
-Corita Kent*

****

PART 1

CRAFTSMANSHIP

"The Mulberry Tree" Painting by Hirschten

THE CHERRY TREE

Audience: All Ages

Once upon a time there was an artist. He traveled the world with everything he owned on this back. In his large sack there were brushes and delicate papers to paint on. Anytime he saw a grand mountain or a quiet river he would sit down and paint it. The artist loved to draw things of beauty.

One day he walked into a city. In the hustle and bustle of the market place, the artist pulled out some of his paintings and displayed them on the corner of a street for sale. Soon soldiers from the emperor's palace came marching by. One of them saw the artist's work and stopped to look at it. "You should come see the emperor," said the soldier. "He is looking for an artist to paint the cherry blossoms that are blooming in the royal garden."

So the artist packed up his things and followed the soldiers to the emperor's palace. There he was taken to the royal garden where a beautiful cherry tree was heavy with pink blooms. The artist stared at the tree for some time until the emperor arrived. "Can you paint my tree, young man?" asked the emperor. "I want to enjoy it all year long and not just for the few days it is in bloom." "I can paint this tree for you, sir," said the artist. "But it will take me a whole year to work on the project. Can you wait that long?" "I can," laughed the emperor. "Good things come to those who wait."

The artist left the palace and traveled to a remote mountain hut. There he painted the cherry tree. Spring ended. Summer, fall and winter passed. When the snow had melted and the buds on the cherry tree opened to the spring warmth again, the artist returned to the palace.

The emperor was sitting at his throne. The artist bowed to him. Then, taking the sack off of his back, he took out his paints, brushes and paper. With agile brush strokes the artist painted the softness of the cherry tree onto a blank sheet of paper. Within a few minutes he was finished. He presented the painting to the emperor and bowed again. The emperor stood up. Sneering, he said, "What is the meaning of this? You said that it would take you a year to paint my cherry tree and yet you have finished it in minutes. You have tricked me and I refuse to pay you."

"No, wait!" said the artist. "This project has taken me a year and I can prove it. Follow me." The emperor and his soldiers followed the artist out of the city to the hut where the artist had worked for a year. Piled high to the ceiling were hundreds of copies of the cherry tree painting. "You see," said the artist. "I had to practice painting the tree. I had to practice until I got it right."

The emperor studied his own copy of the painting and then sighed. "It is my tree. And it will keep blooming throughout the year," said the emperor. "You have captured the spirit of the tree and I thank you for it."

Thoughts: The value of a work of art is not simply the time put into it or the cost of the materials. Craftsmanship is derived from sincere study and devotion. Over and over again we create in order to find the sweet spot where we are clearly communicating the message of the artwork to the viewer. In the case of the "Cherry Tree" story, the message of the artwork was to express admiration for the delicately beautiful tree. The value artists bring to the table is their ability to open our eyes, to shed light on what we value and transform our world. You can use art to transform your space into a place where there is more beauty, more justice... more of whatever you want.

Source: This is a folktale of Asian origin told to me by a teacher in high school. I have not been able to find another documentation of it so if this is familiar to you please let me know where you heard it! As an adult I couldn't remember what object the artist painted over and over for a year. Inspired by the many beautiful Japanese watercolor paintings of cherry trees, I decided to make that the subject depicted.

Classroom Ideas: Pair this story with a study on Japanese Sumi-e ink paintings or on Monet's Impressionist paintings of the haystacks and Rouen Cathedral.

****

"Let the beauty we love be what we do. There are hundreds of ways to kneel and kiss the ground."
-Rumi

****

"The Violin" Painting by Hirschten

FLANNERY'S DREAM

Audience: All Ages

Once upon a time there was a man named Flannery. One day he went over to the house of a friend so that they could play fiddle together. The two musicians found that they knew many of the same songs. Jokingly, Flannery said "I bet

I know more tunes than you do." They created a list, finding that they both knew the exact same number of tunes. The friend challenged Flannery to come back the next day. If he had thought of any more songs he would declare Flannery "the best fiddle player in the county."

Flannery went home. He sat by the fire with his fiddle and bow at hand ready to play any new songs he could think of. He thought and he thought until his head drooped, his shoulders sagged and he drifted off to sleep.

In his dream Flannery flew through the air. His feet wafted the clouds. He felt the wind gently pushing past his body. Suddenly he saw mountains below. He flew toward them, almost touching the top of each crest. There was a cave. From the cave emerged a bear that had just woken from his hibernation slumber. The bear lumbered up and down the mountains, down into the valleys and up again to the ridges. Flannery heard music drifting in the air. The bear was now walking upright like a human, playing a fiddle and chasing after Flannery. The bear danced around the mountains, his music echoing through the trees.

Flannery woke up with a start. He remembered the tune the bear had been playing. Picking up his fiddle he played the tune for himself then ran to his friend's house.

Excitedly Flannery played the tune for his friend. The friend had never heard it before. Flannery had thought of another tune and the friend hadn't. Flannery won the bet. They decided to call this new tune "Flannery's Dream" and went on to share it with many other musicians who continue to play it to this day.

Thoughts: Inspiration comes to those who wait patiently, allowing the creative juice of dreams to spill forth.

Source: This is a folktale from the old-time music scene in Kentucky. Many fiddlers have recorded this tune. I especially love Bruce Greene's version.

Classroom Ideas: The images from this tale are so vivid that I've simply asked young students to illustrate it. Also I've performed this story with another fiddler. We acted out the story, playing tunes for the audience and used a "Cranky" shadow puppet theater to create the dream sequence.

****

"What is laid down, ordered, factual, is never enough to embrace the whole truth; life always spills over the rim of every cup."
-Boris Pasternak

****

"The Strawberry Thief" Design by William Morris

WILLIAM MORRIS AND
THE ARTS AND CRAFTS MOVEMENT

Audience: All Ages

In England during the 1860s William Morris and his fellow artists started a revolution that is now known as the Arts and Crafts Movement. Before that time "fine art" was work that could be put on a pedestal, work that was for viewing only. By definition art was not a part of everyday life but for the prestigious enjoyment of the wealthy. New machines were mass producing more and more household items. Cups, silverware, and fabrics were being created by machines in what Morris and his friends thought were boring, bland designs.

Morris decided that he wanted everything in his house to be both useful and beautiful. He campaigned for the arts to include pottery, furniture, and household items. He became a successful fabric and wallpaper designer using patterns inspired by nature. He believed that "art is not for the few, any more than education is for the few or freedom for a few." He wanted every person, rich or poor, to be surrounded by the beauty of nature and in turn the beauty of art.

Thoughts: The most important lesson to be learned from William Morris' life work is that we have the power to bring beauty into our lives in whatever way we choose. If there is an ugly alleyway, you can make it a garden. If there is a plain whitewashed wall in your child's school, you can make it a mural. As Rumi said, "in the garden there are no distinctions." There is no distinction between art on the wall or the hand thrown mug you are drinking coffee from. It is all from the same source. The materials used to make art are not as important as the value it brings to our lives.

Source: This is a true story. Read *"The Beauty of Life: William Morris and the Art of Design"* edited by Diane Waggoner. It is one of my dreams to tour Morris' home, *"Red House,"* in London.

Classroom Ideas: Study the designs of William Morris. Challenge students to create their own wallpaper design. Brainstorm ways in which the students could bring artistic flare into their homes.

****

"The past is not dead. It is living in us and will be alive in the future we are now helping to create."
-William Morris

****

"Time for Bed" Illustration by Hirschten

THE MOON AND THE DRESSMAKER

Audience: All Ages

Once upon a time there was a dressmaker who worked hard at constructing the most stylish outfits in the village. She had a long list of clients who were waiting for her to make new clothes for them. She often worked late into the night to complete as many projects as possible.

One evening she was leaning over her work table cutting out pieces for the princess's next ball gown when she heard a whisper say, "Dear dressmaker, please make me a gown of

33

the finest silk."

The dressmaker looked up. High in the sky the moon gazed down upon her. The moon smiled and asked again, "Please dressmaker, please make me a gown of the finest silk."

The dressmaker thought for a moment then shook her head. "How could I ever make you a gown? One day you are round and then you get smaller and smaller until you are just a sliver. Then you change back again. No, I'm sorry Moon but you change too often for me to make a gown that would properly fit you."

The moon sighed sadly. The dressmaker comforted her, saying, "Do not worry, my dear, everyone thinks you are beautiful just as you are." And with that the dressmaker leaned over her work and began pushing the needle through the fabric once again.

Thoughts: As artists we create works of art to suit many purposes. Sometimes we create for personal art therapy. Sometimes we create to honor nature. Sometimes we create to make a political statement. These are all valid reasons to create art, but sometimes we confuse our audience when the purpose of our work changes too often. Sometimes we even confuse ourselves! In order to improve at our craft it can be helpful to focus, narrowing down our purpose.

Source: Written by the Greek author, Aesop, circa 600BC.

Classroom Ideas: Challenge your adult students to write an artist statement that clearly defines what type of art they create and why. Children can brainstorm reasons to make artwork. How does the finished product fit the needs of the viewer?

****

"Quality is better than quantity."
-Aesop

****

"Father and Son Fishing" Painting by Hirschten

THE THREE BROTHERS

Audience: All Ages

Once upon a time there was an old man who had three sons. They all lived and worked together on a farm. One day the father picked up a bucket of water and strained his back. It took him several days to heal. He realized that his body was getting old. He decided that he needed to declare which of his sons would inherit the farm after he died.

Each of his sons had strengths and weaknesses. The

37

father did not know which one would be the best choice, so he decided that they would have a competition.

The father gathered his sons together and said, "You see that barn over there. We are going to empty it. I want each of you to try to fill the empty space with just one type of thing. Whichever of you fills it the best will be in charge of the farm after I have passed away."

The first son loved animals. So he gathered up every single animal on the farm and stuffed them into the barn. The chickens squawked. The cows mooed. The pigs oinked. It was a loud riot inside that barn but the animals only filled six feet worth of space in the air.

They emptied the barn of the animals. The second brother went to the fields and harvested all of the hay. He baled it into squares and stacked the hay in the barn. It filled the barn all the way up to the rafters, but there was still some air space at the very top of the ceiling.

They emptied the barn of hay. Then the third brother went in. He was able to fill the space in an instant. He took his flute and played a song. The sound of his music drifted up into the barn filling every nook and cranny. The brothers and their father listened to the sweet sound. It filled the barn and their souls.

The father decided that the third son had won the competition. He would inherit the farm.

Thoughts: I see the barn as a metaphor for the human body. The animals and hay could represent food and water. We need those items to physically stay alive, yet it is the arts that fill our souls.

Source: This riddle tale is found in several European countries. Sometimes the answer is a candle of light and other times it is a musical instrument. My favorite read-aloud version is the book, "*The Three Brothers*," by Carolyn Croll. The Grimm Brothers documented a story by the same title but the outcome is quite different.

Classroom Ideas: I love to pause the story right before the third brother enters the barn to allow the students to guess what he will bring in. I hint that "he filled the space in an instant." Often they will guess abstract concepts like "love." If that happens after the story has been resolved I say that maybe he was expressing "love" through his music. Then we can expand to talk about what we are trying to express when we make art together.

****

"All art is but an imitation of our nature."
-Seneca

****

"My Daughter and the Kite" Painting by Hirschten

THE KITE STORY

Audience: All Ages

One day a group of students made kites in art class. Once they had decorated them and attached the string, they rushed outside to test how well the kites would fly. Even though it was a very windy day, none of the kites would stay in the air. They would spin, then plop back to the ground. One student's parents piped in to say that there was too much wind. It would be best to wait until the wind died down. "But we need wind for the kites to fly," exclaimed one of the children. The mother shook her head. "Trust me, I've flown many kites over the years. You can't have too much or too little wind. It has to be just right."

The children were sad. Some thought it was the design of their kites that was to blame. When they returned the next day, however, the kites caught the wind just fine.

Thoughts: It is common to "blow too much wind" on creative projects. The timing must be right for them to come to successful fruition. Be patient.

Source: This is a true story that the author witnessed in 2012.

Classroom Ideas: Create kites and design the exterior decorations. One interesting topic is kite designs from Afghanistan. Many kite designers there incorporate political messages into their decoration. Some groups there have tried to suppress this form of freedom of speech. What similar messages would your students like to share?

****

"Be gentle, for you know not what you may be killing with too much forcing."
-Jenny Read

****

PART 2

ALCHEMY AND TRANSFORMATION

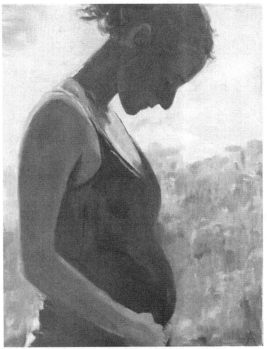

"Now There is a Pearl" Illustration by Hirschten

PYGMALION

Audience: All Ages

Once upon a time there was a sculptor named Pygmalion. This man studied in the finest art schools and crafted his work until he was known as the best sculptor in the land. He would wake in the morning and carve images into stone until late at night. He bragged to his friends that the reason he was so successful was because he didn't do anything else. He didn't even want to marry a wife because he thought a woman would distract him from his work.

One day he bought a large piece of marble. The stone was perfectly smooth and creamy. Pygmalion carved into the marble the form of a woman. When he finished he stepped back to look at her. She was perfectly beautiful. Pygmalion stared at this sculpture for a long time. He imagined that she was real. He wanted for her to be real. He thought that if such a perfect woman existed he would marry her.

Time passed and every day Pygmalion would sit and stare at this sculpture. He forgot his job. He forgot his friends. His love for the sculpture grew until finally Venus, the goddess of love, noticed his pain.

Venus whispered in Pygmalion's ear, "Kiss her." He rose, walked to the sculpture and touched his lips to hers. When he did he found that they were not hard and cold, but soft as flesh. Pygmalion found that his sculpture had been changed into a real woman. She wrapped her arms around him and returned his kiss. Venus had made the sculpture real.

Pygmalion married the woman. They raised a family and lived happily ever after.

Thoughts: We each have the power to create our own reality. We don't need the touch of a goddess. We can breathe life into our creations through our actions.

There is also a message in this story about the importance of being true to our nature. Repressing our instincts in favor of being a workaholic creates imbalance.

Source: This is a Greek myth recounted in Ovid's *"Metamorphosis"* written in the year 8 AD. Many renditions of this story have been written, including the movies, *"My Fair Lady"* and *"Mannequin."*

Classroom Ideas: Pair this story with a study on Greek sculpture.

****

"To love is to recognize yourself in another."
-Eckhart Tolle

****

"Capaneus the Blasphemer from Dante's Divine Comedy" Illustration by William Blake

FRANKENSTEIN

Audience: Age 8 and up

Once upon a time there was a young scientist named Victor Frankenstein. When his mother died of scarlet fever Frankenstein decided to create an "elixir of life." If he could perfect this technique he would be able to keep people alive forever. None of his loved ones would ever die again.

Frankenstein hid within his castle. He experimented with dead bodies and lightening until he was successful. He created a creature formed out of many corpses. It was 8 feet tall and monstrous in appearance. By channeling a bolt of lightning into the body, the monster sprang to life. Frankenstein ran away in fear of the hideous creature. Confused, the monster ran off. Frankenstein had created a creature he could not control.

A few months later Frankenstein's brother was found murdered. A woman was charged with the crime and hanged. Frankenstein feared that his creature was the true murderer.

Roaming through the woods, the monster found Frankenstein. He explained how horrible it was that everyone was afraid of him. The monster feared that people would hurt him. He taught himself to read and write in the hopes that he would be able to talk to people. Frankenstein was still afraid of his creature and fled.

The monster found a small house where a family lived. He approached them hoping to become their friend but the family ran away in terror. The monster became angry because he was so misunderstood. He burned down the family's house in retaliation.

The monster hunted down Frankenstein again. This time he demanded that the scientist make a female creature like himself so that he would have a companion. Frankenstein went to a remote island in Scotland to create the female. As he was working Frankenstein became afraid of what would happen to humans if the two monsters worked together. Frankenstein destroyed the female form he had been working on. When the monster found out he took vengeance by killing Frankenstein's good friend Clerval. Frankenstein was blamed for the murder.

Frankenstein returned home to marry a woman named Elizabeth. It was difficult for the scientist to enjoy his honeymoon, however, because he was worried that the monster would return to murder again. Frankenstein left Elizabeth to hunt for the monster. After searching and searching he returned home without finding him. Upon entering his castle he found that Elizabeth had been killed by the monster while he was away. Frankenstein decided that the monster must be destroyed and traveled to the North Pole in search of him.

Frankenstein died on the voyage north. The monster soon appeared on the ship where Frankenstein's body lay motionless. The monster mourned over the scientist's body and told the captain that he would kill himself. He got on a raft and drifted out to sea, disappearing into the darkness.

Thoughts: When artists create they are often afraid of the impact that their creations will have. Will their work be understood? Will others think the artist is crazy? Do not let your fear of losing control of what others think of your art stop you from moving forward. Focus on making positive work. The fear of our creations is a fear of ourselves and our own power.

Source: This is an adaptation of a story written by Mary Shelley in 1814. She and her friends had a competition to see who could write the best horror story. It is said that she was inspired by an alchemist named Johann Dippel. He hunted for an elixir of life 200 years earlier while living in the Frankenstein Castle in Germany.

Classroom Ideas: I love prompting the class with the question of what they would do if they had the "elixir of life." Another option is to ask what they are most afraid of. Did they create the situation that they are afraid of? How can they confront that demon?

****

"Beauty awakens the soul to act."
- Dante

****

"David" Sculpture by Michelangelo

MICHELANGELO'S DAVID

Audience: All Ages

In the year 1464 an artist by the name of Agostino was commissioned to create a large sculpture. He worked under the master craftsman Donatello for the Florence Cathedral in Italy. It would be an image of the biblical character, David. Agostino started carving out the legs of the sculpture but did not get very far along in the project. When Donatello died in

1466 Agostino left the enormous block of marble in the yard of the cathedral's workshop. It sat out in the wind and the rain for thirty-five years.

In 1501 the young artist Michelangelo saw the piece of marble neglected in the yard and begged to complete the sculpture of David. He was awarded a contract and worked on the project for over two years. The finished sculpture is considered a masterpiece of craftsmanship. David holds a rock in his hand, his glaring eyes ready to fight the giant Goliath. The determined look on his face makes it easy for us to envision him defeating the giant. The statue is fourteen feet tall and weighs over six tons! It is ironic that the character David was small compared to the giant Goliath. Now it is David who towers over visitors to the sculpture when they visit it in Florence.

Thoughts: It is said that "one man's junk is another man's treasure." The lesson to be learned from this story is to always be on the lookout for materials that are right under your nose, perhaps neglected by others. From those treasures masterpieces can be formed.

Source: This is a true story. A. Victor Coonin sorts through the legends and facts about the creation of this sculpture in the book, "*From Marble to Flesh: The Biography of Michelangelo's David.*"

Classroom Ideas: Create your own depictions of the character David. This could be done with sculpture or drawing. Children especially love making his counterpart, Goliath, as well.

****

"The sculptor's hand can break the spell to free the figures slumbering in the stone."
-Michelangelo

****

"Apple Reflections" Painting by Hirschten

THE VINEGAR BOTTLE

Audience: All Ages

Once upon a time there was a woman who inherited a piece of land out in the woods. When she arrived on the spot she found that there was no house for her to live in. For several days she slept out under the stars, shivering in the cold. Luckily, a hiker walked by. Out of his sack fell a large green glass bottle. "I could make this my home," thought the woman. She squeezed herself inside the bottle.

While the woman brought rugs and pillows into the bottle and tried to make it as comfy as possible, it was still a cramped abode. She sat outside her house sighing to herself and said, "What a pity it is that I live in this teeny-tiny green glass bottle. I wish I could live in a cozy county cottage with a thatched roof and roses climbing up around the door. If I had that, I would be happy." The woman did not know it but a little fairy sat upon her shoulder. The fairy declared, "If that is what she wants, that is what she can have." In an instant the bottle was replaced with a cozy country cottage with a thatched roof and roses climbing up around the door. The woman was ecstatically happy. The fairy flew away.

The fairy flew to the north. She flew to the south. She flew to the east and she flew to the west. A few weeks later she came to sit upon the woman's shoulder again. This time the woman was saying to herself, "What a pity it is that I live in this small country cottage. I wish I lived in a golden palace with servants to help me cook and clean. If I had that, I would be happy." The fairy declared, "If that is what she wants, that is what she can have." In an instant the cottage was replaced with a golden palace. It had servants and a horse drawn carriage to take the woman anywhere she wanted to go. The woman was ecstatically happy. The fairy flew away.

The fairy flew to the north. She flew to the south. She flew to the east and she flew to the west. A few weeks later she came to sit upon the woman's shoulder again. This time the woman was saying to herself, "What a pity it is that I am not queen of the land. If I were in charge, the kingdom would run so smoothly." The fairy declared, "If that is what she wants, that is what she can have." In an instant the woman had a sparkly crown placed atop her head. She was queen of the land. The woman was ecstatically happy. The fairy flew away.

The fairy flew to the north. She flew to the south. She flew to the east and she flew to the west. A few weeks later she came to sit upon the woman's shoulder again. This time the woman was saying to herself, "What a pity it is that the sun rises so early in the morning and sets so late at night. The stars could be more twinkly. The moon could be more luminescent. I wish I was queen of the sun and the moon and the stars." "Oh no!" thought the fairy. "No one can be queen of the sun and the moon and the stars." The fairy hung her head in sorrow. In an instant the woman was placed back where she had started. She had only a green glass bottle for a home. She had used up all of the wishes of her good fairy because of her selfishness.

Thoughts: Just as it is not possible for all of our wishes to come true, it is not possible to do all of our creative endeavors. Carefully select your creative projects so that you do not run out of steam. We make our wishes come true with our own hard work.

Source: This is a folktale from Britain. Another of my favorite versions is *"The Old Woman Who Lived in a Vinegar Bottle"* by Margaret Read MacDonald. I combined elements of *"The Vinegar Bottle"* story with another folktale, *"The Magic Fish."*

Classroom Ideas: This story is about being selective with our wishes and grateful for what we have already earned. Have adult students create a list of art projects that they would like to complete along with one listing what they have already accomplished. Ask them to prioritize the future list so that they can be selective with their most important goals. Ask children to brainstorm realistic wishes that they could fulfill. Talk about the difference between unrealistic goals and obtainable ones.

****

"Everything you can imagine is real."
-Picasso

****

"Charlottenburg Palace" Painting by Hirschten

KING MIDAS

Audience: All Ages

Once upon a time there was a king. He woke up one morning, yawned, stretched, and looked out his window. It was a perfect, clear summer morning. He decided to take a walk before breakfast.

Opening the doors, he stepped out onto the terrace and made his way down the steps into the garden. He wandered down the hill, passing the roses in bloom, until he reached the river.

Looking out over the river, the king saw the sun glistening on the water. A raft carrying a little boy moved swiftly with the current. The raft hit a rock. The boy fell into the water and started flailing about. The king knew he must act fast or the boy would drown. Diving into the water, the king grabbed the boy and pulled him to safety. Back on dry land the boy coughed up some water but was fine. The boy headed home, walking along the shore back to his village.

When the king turned back to the palace, he was startled to find a tall green genie standing before him. "King Midas," said the genie. "You have performed a very good deed. For that I will grant you one wish. Any wish your heart desires. What would you like to wish for?"

Now the king had many things... a palace, a daughter, servants to help him, plenty of food and peace in the land. He could think of nothing that he didn't already have. Maybe he could wish for more of his favorite things? His mind went to his crown and his jewelry. He loved how these items were made of gold. He loved how the hard, shiny metal reflected the warm glow of light when it was touched by the sun. The king decided that he wanted for everything he owned to be gold.

"Genie," said King Midas. "I wish for everything I touch to be turned to gold." The genie bowed his head, smiled and declared, "Your wish is granted." Then, poof, the genie was gone.

King Midas looked at his hands. Would this magic work? Had his wish truly been granted? Lowering his hand to the sand of the shore he placed it flat on the ground. When he lifted it up again, he found that every grain of sand he had touched glittered in the sun. The handprint was of solid gold!

Excited now, King Midas ran up the hill toward the palace. As he ran he touched a tree. It turned to gold. He touched a rosebush. It turned to gold. He touched one of the steps leading up to the terrace. It turned to gold. He opened the door. It turned to gold. Smiling to himself he thought, "I'll turn my whole palace to gold after I eat my breakfast."

Entering the dining hall, the king sat on his thrown. It turned to gold. He picked up his glass. It turned to gold. Lifting the glass to his lips, he took a sip of the water. It turned to gold. He was forced to spit it out. "Oh dear," thought the king. "I can't drink." He lifted his spoon. It turned to gold. Placing the porridge in his mouth, it turned to gold.

At that moment his daughter ran into the room. "Daddy!" she said. "Yesterday this rose was soft and red. Now it is hard and yellow. What has happened?" The king turned to answer his daughter's question. He touched her shoulder. She turned to gold.

The king shook his daughter in disbelief, but she remained still as a statue. "Genie! Genie!!!" cried the king. "Please come back. I don't want the gift of the golden touch any longer. Help!"

In an instant, poof, the genie returned. "King Midas," said the genie, "I thought you might change your mind about this wish. Never fear, take your daughter back down to the river. When she is dunked in the water she will return to normal. Then you can wash your hands clean of the golden touch."

"Oh, thank you!" cried the king. Grabbing his daughter, he ran down the steps to the river. She was thrown into the water and awoke with a start. She didn't know she had been a statue. Then the king lowered his hands into the water. At first, flecks of gold floated off of his fingers. As the king scrubbed his hands together, however, the golden touch was eventually washed away.

The king and his daughter returned to the palace and lived happily ever after.

Thoughts: When we create anything, we are participating in the powerful act of transformation. This is "the alchemy of art." Magic is not needed for our wishes to come true if we take action to fulfill them. Even in the ordinary world, however, we must be careful what we wish for. Material items are only the shell for things of true value.

Source: This is an ancient Greek myth found in Ovid's "*Metamorphosis*." The American author, Nathaniel Hawthorne, added the daughter to the story.

Classroom Ideas: Nothing is more fun than asking a group of students what they would wish for. When performing this story I often stop right before King Midas makes his wish to ask the audience what they would choose. Take this one step further by asking the students to draw their wishes.

****

"To be of use to the world is the only way to be happy."
-Hans Christian Andersen

****

PART 3

WHAT IS BEAUTY?

"Picture of Dorian Gray" Painting by Hirschten

THE PICTURE OF DORIAN GRAY

Audience: Age 8 and up

Once upon a time there was a handsome young man named Dorian Gray. He was asked by an artist to sit for a portrait painting because the artist admired his youthful beauty so much. When the artist was finished with the portrait, Dorian Gray looked at the painting. He became sad realizing that the painting would look young forever, while he would slowly become old and gray. Dorian said to himself, "I wish I could stay young forever and that the portrait would get old instead." By some strange magic Dorian's wish came true.

Dorian soon realized that the portrait was aging and not his body. It aged especially fast whenever he did an evil deed, twisting the features of the face. The deformed face in the portrait reflected the image of Dorian's soul. Unfortunately Dorian made more and more bad choices. No one believed that he was evil, however, because his face looked so young and innocent. The portrait became monstrous in appearance. Dorian hid the portrait in his attic so that no one would discover the secret to his prolonged youth.

Dorian blamed the evil corruption of his soul on the painting. He decided to take revenge on the artist who created it by stabbing the painter to death. Then Dorian blackmailed another friend into destroying the body. This crime turned the figure in the painting into an even more grotesque form.

Dorian tried to reform his actions. He longed to become a better person, but for selfish reasons. When he did something nice for someone else, he didn't perform the kind act to help that person but to change the painting. The portrait remained the same. Tormented by the painting Dorian decided to destroy it using the same knife he had used to kill the artist. He went upstairs to the attic where he kept the painting. He stabbed it with the knife and then doubled over in pain himself. The servants came running to the scene when they heard Dorian's cries of pain. They forced the door open they found an aged and monstrous old man dead on the floor, a knife in his stomach. Mysteriously the painting reverted to its original form: an image of Dorian Gray, young and innocent.

Thoughts: Inner beauty doesn't necessarily match outer beauty in a person. We are often swayed by the appearance of things. It is important to not put too much stock in visual beauty.

When artists create work it is often said that the images are a reflection of their soul or inner conscience. What does your artwork say about your inner thoughts and feelings?

Source: This story was written by Oscar Wilde in 1891. Wilde considered himself to be an aesthete, someone who loves beauty. When he wrote this novella he was questioning the importance of beauty and how we judge others.

Classroom Ideas: Ask the students to draw a picture of how they wished they looked or a portrait of their soul. Ask how it would be different or the same as their own physical image.

****

"The moment one gives close attention to anything, even a blade of grass, it becomes a mysterious, awesome, indescribably magnificent world in itself."
-Henry Miller

****

"The Mona Lisa" Painting by Leonardo da Vinci

THE MONA LISA

Audience: All Ages

Around the year 1503 Leonardo da Vinci created the famous painting "The Mona Lisa." It depicts a gently smiling woman with her hands neatly folded in front of her. The woman was most likely Lisa Gherardini, the wife of a wealthy silk merchant. Mona is a shortened version of "Ma Donna" meaning "My Lady" in Old Italian. Modern Italians, however, call the painting "La Gioconda," meaning "The Happy One."

"The Mona Lisa" was bought by the French King Francois I after da Vinci died in 1519. It later became a part of the Louvre Art Museum's collection in France.

The painting was admired by many people but didn't truly become famous until its mysterious theft in 1911. A painter, Louis Beroud, came to the Louvre to visit the "Mona Lisa" painting only to discover that there was an empty spot on the wall where the painting should have been. He contacted the security guards, who assumed that the painting had been taken for photographing. It was then discovered that the painting was missing. The Louvre shut its doors for a week to try to solve the crime.

Grasping at straws, the authorities accused a French poet by the name of Guillaume Apollinaire for the theft. Apollinaire had once stated that the Louvre should be burned down. They assumed this was an act of revenge against the museum. Apollinaire was arrested and imprisoned. Apollinaire accused another artist, Pablo Picasso, of the crime. Picasso was brought in for questioning. Eventually both Picasso and Apollinaire were found innocent.

The true culprit of the crime was finally discovered two years later in 1913. The thief, Vincenzo Peruggia, tried to sell the painting to an Italian art museum. He was caught and sentenced to six months imprisonment. He had been able to steal the painting when he was working for the Louvre as an employee. He had simply hidden it under his coat and walked out the back door. When asked why he did it Peruggia claimed that he believed the painting belonged in his homeland of Italy.

You can now visit the "Mona Lisa" in the Louvre Museum. It is protected under bulletproof glass.

Thoughts: People are drawn to the pleasant expression on the "Mona Lisa's" face. She has become a mysterious woman, both because the painting was stolen and because we know so little about the real woman who sat for the portrait. Art is a visual language that we use to express the subtle emotions that cannot be put into words. The content of the "Mona Lisa's" character is visible to us yet mysterious.

Source: This is a true story. Read *"Mona Lisa: A Life*

Discovered" for a glimpse into what life may have been like for the original Lisa Gherardini who lived in Renaissance Italy.

Classroom Ideas: Have your students meditate on the image of the "Mona Lisa" and then write a story about her. Or you can have the students create portraits of each other inspired by the original painting.

****

"Art does not reproduce the visible, but makes visible that which is not easily seen."
-Kimon Nikolaides

****

"Foxgloves in my Garden" Painting by Hirschten

BLOOM WHERE YOU ARE PLANTED

Audience: All Ages

When I was a teenager I became obsessed with France. It began when I started taking French language classes. I read French literature. I watched French movies. I ate French food. I read about the bold style of Impressionist art. I tacked French art posters all over the walls of my bedroom. I listened to language tapes over and over. Finally, the day came when I was to travel to France to be an exchange student.

When I arrived I found that there were many wonderful things about France. My host family owned a seafood restaurant called "Le Fruit de la Mer [The Fruit of the Sea]." They served me five course meals every evening. I didn't even need butter on my bread because the bread was so good by itself.

There was trouble in paradise, however. Our group had numerous delays due to train problems, traffic and strikes in the streets. It was very gray there. Perhaps because of all of the French paintings I had looked at, I had imagined a colorful, almost tropical place. The sun did not shine his happy face often during the fall when I was there. I also still had all my old aches and pains. If I stubbed my toe in France it hurt just as much as it had back home.

Toward the end of my stay, I took a day trip down to Paris with a group. I was feeling melancholy, sad that my journey was almost over and deep down disappointed that my French utopia wasn't all it was cracked up to be. I was looking at the ground and darting around the rain puddles. We came to an intersection. I looked up to see where I was going. Across the street there was a second story apartment window. Hanging from that window was a large banner. In English the banner read: "Bloom where you are planted."

Thoughts: Often happiness feels like it is just out of reach. It is as if we are climbing a mountain trying to reach the summit of bliss but the mountain just gets taller. It feels as though Utopia is just over the next crest of the hill but remains elusive. If we can accept where we are we can learn to 'bloom' anywhere. We can learn to create happiness by allowing our roots to sink down into the soil of wherever the wind takes us. We can learn to be thankful for what we have.

If you can love one person, you can love yourself. If you can love yourself, you can love anyone. If you can see the beauty in one spot on earth, you can see it anywhere.

Source: This is a personal story by the author.

Classroom Ideas: Share this story when doing a painting study of flowers. Or have the students design their own Utopian city. When they are finished ask them to think of ways that their own home already has the qualities they seek.

****

"The whole world is a single flower."
-Seung Sahn

****

"De Colores" Painting by Hirschten

THE STONE FLOWER

Audience: All Ages

Once upon a time there was an orphan named Danny. He was taken in by a kind man who worked as a stone carver. As he grew up, Danny learned from his new father how to create jewelry made of stone. When he grew to be young man, Danny met someone who made his heart sing. It was a woman named Katya.

Danny asked Katya to marry him. The date was set for the wedding. Danny decided to make Katya a special gift for the occasion. Finding a large chunk of green malachite he carved a vase with a flower design winding up the side. When he was finished, he was displeased, however, because he thought the flowers lacked the natural gracefulness of real flowers. He longed to make the vase as beautiful as his Katya.

His father laughed when he heard of Danny's struggle designing the vase. "You should find the mythical 'Stone Flower' for inspiration," his father said. "It grows up on Copper Mountain but the old folks say it will ensnare you… so be careful!"

The moment Danny heard his father's words he put on his shoes and coat to make the long journey up the mountain to find the Stone Flower. After many days of travel Danny found a glen where gems glittered on the ground. A shaft of light pierced through the branches of the trees, shining upon the Stone Flower. As his eyes gazed up at it, the Stone Flower enchanted Danny, clouding his judgment. He thought he had never before seen anything so beautiful. Falling to his knees he worshiped the flower, forgetting both his father and Katya.

Time passed. As Danny sat worshiping the flower his father became ill and died. Katya worried and wondered if Danny was lost or hurt. Everyone urged Katya to forget Danny but she could not. After three years, Katya decided to go look for him.

She wandered far and wide, asking everyone if they had seen Danny. After she had visited every village, Katya decided that he must have gone where no one dared to live, up in the lonely hills of Copper Mountain.

Finally Katya found the glen with glittering gems and Danny enchanted by the stone flower. When she touched Danny's arm, the spell was broken. He looked up, blinked and could see again. He remembered his love for Katya. Looking down at the flower he realized that for all its beauty the Stone Flower could never love him back. Danny and Katya left the glen. Traveling back down the mountain they went home.

Thoughts: Sometimes artists get wrapped up in the hunt for perfection with their craftsmanship. It is important to remember that the gift of art to the receiver is more important than elusive perfection. In a painting we cannot depict every leaf on a tree. When throwing a pot we cannot create a perfect sphere. Yet it is in the imperfections that art becomes graceful, like nature. If "it is the thought that counts," what thought is the artist trying to convey?

Source: This is an adaptation of a Russian tale by Pavel Bazhov set in the Ural Mountains. It was also made into a ballet composed by Sergei Prokofiev.

Classroom Ideas: Challenge your students to make a gift for someone they love. Ask them to make it "as beautiful as that person." What image would symbolize that person?

****

"It is the time you have wasted for your rose that makes your rose so important."
-Antoine de Saint-Exupery, "The Little Prince"

****

"The Spider Web Painting by Hirschten

THE SILKWORM WEAVER

Audience: All Ages

Once upon a time a silkworm was commissioned by the Princess of the land to weave a silk tapestry. The tapestry would be displayed in the grand hall of the palace. The silkworm worked tirelessly at the job over many days and nights, until one evening her friend the spider came to visit her.

The spider paced back and forth, admiring the silkworm's

fabric. Finally she jumped up to the corner of the room. "I can make a finer weave than you, Ms. Silkworm," she declared.

The spider quickly wove a delicate web in the corner of the room. "Done!" said the spider. "I worked faster than you as well."

The silkworm looked up at the web. "You did a fine job and you did work quickly, Sister Spider. But your weave is made only to be a trap for insects and it will last only a few days. My tapestry will be admired for many years to come."

Thoughts: It is often tempting to work quickly to get a task done as fast as possible. Yet when we do this, we cheat ourselves out of the satisfaction of a job well done. It is worth taking your time, doing it right, and making a piece of lasting beauty.

Source: This story was written by the Greek author Aesop circa 600BC.

Classroom Ideas: Encourage your students to slow down. One trick is to stop the project. Force them to stare at their piece for five minutes. In that time they may formulate better decisions than if they had blindly charged ahead.

****

"Invisible threads make the strongest ties."
-Nietzsche

****

PART 4

THANKFULNESS

"The Cliffs of La Jolla" Painting by Hirschten

THE STRAWBERRY

Audience: All Ages

Once upon a time a young man was walking through the jungle playing his flute. He was fantasizing about seeing his girlfriend that evening. He imagined that she would be amazed when she heard the new song he was playing.

Suddenly he heard the crunch of a footstep behind him. Turning the man looked into the face of a tiger who was stalking him.

Dropping his instrument, he ran as fast as he could until he reached a cliff. He jumped over the edge and grabbed hold of a tree half-way down the mountain. Looking up he could see the tiger above him. Looking down he saw another tiger that was pacing, waiting for him to fall.

The man turned his head to the rocks. He noticed that there was a wild strawberry growing out of the jagged cliff. The strawberry was heavy with juice and warm from the sun. He plucked the strawberry and ate it. It was the most wonderful thing he had ever eaten in his whole entire life.

The end.

Thoughts: The first time I read this story I hated it! I wanted to know what happened to our young man. Is he going to live or die? It is literally a 'cliff-hanger' and I craved resolution for this story. Then I learned that this is a Buddhist koan. A koan is a story meant to teach a spiritual lesson. A Buddhist friend explained to me that the tiger above represents past suffering and that the tiger below represents future suffering. The strawberry is the present moment which is always there for our enjoyment if we can just turn our heads to view it. Perhaps the young man could have avoided the tigers altogether if he had let go of the fantasy of impressing his girlfriend in the future. He could have been thankful for that moment. He could have enjoyed playing his music for only the jungle to hear.

This story grew on me and now it is one of my favorites.

Source: This is a traditional Buddhist koan story.

Classroom Ideas: When working with adults I challenge them to give up their goals of creating the perfect artwork for someone else. While it is fine to create work for the purpose of sharing with others, if the root of the artwork is in ego gratification the work will only lead to suffering.

When working with kids I ask them to illustrate the story. What symbol can they use to help them to remember to enjoy the present moment other than a strawberry? Then those symbols are incorporated into their artwork for the day.

****

"Eagerly savor each new day and the taste of its mouth. Never lose sight of the thrill and the joy of living."
-Ewan MacColl

****

"The Star and the Flower" Painting by Hirschten

THE STORY OF TANABATA

Audience: All Ages

Once upon a time there was Weaver Princess who worked night and day on her loom creating the tapestry of colors found in the sky. She sat on a cloud surrounded by stars weaving sunrises and sunsets for people to enjoy. She never rested and thought of nothing but her important work.

One day she heard a strange sound from across the stars. It was a large herd of cattle stomping through the sky, led by the handsome Herdsman. When the Weaver Princess saw the Herdsman, she got up from her loom. She ran to greet him. In that moment the two fell in love. They went to the Weaver Princess' father, the Ruler of the Heavens, to ask for permission to marry.

A wedding soon took place. The Weaver Princess and the Herdsman were so happy together that they never left each other's sides. Soon the Ruler of the Heavens noticed that the young couple were neglecting their duties. The Herdsman was allowing his cattle to eat the stars in the sky. The Weaver Princess hadn't created any new colors for the sky. The heavens appeared bleak.

The Ruler of the Heavens separated the couple. He placed the Herdsman on one side of the galaxy and the Weaver Princess on the other. Between them was the Milky Way. The Ruler made the Milky Way fill with water. It roared like a river in the spring. The Weaver Princess and the Herdsman could only cry and wave to each other from afar.

After some time the Ruler of the Heavens took pity on the sad couple. He decided to allow them to meet once a year on the seventh day of the seventh month, as long as they did not neglect their duties the rest of the year.

Now every year on the seventh day of the seventh month, you can look into the night sky to see a blue and a yellow star meet. This is the happy annual reunion of the Weaver Princess and the Herdsman. The time spent apart makes them even more thankful for each other.

Thoughts: We must create balance in our lives between our work, creative endeavors and play. It is not good to be a workaholic; nor is it good to be neglectful of work.

Source: This is an ancient Chinese and Japanese folktale. In Japan the seventh day of the seventh month is celebrated as the star festival of Tanabata. In China it is known as the Qixi Festival.

Classroom Ideas: This story can be a jumping off point for a study of star constellations. Greek mythology also has many constellation stories.

****

*"What good is the warmth of summer,
without the cold of winter to give it
sweetness."
-John Steinbeck*

****

"Hydrangeas" Painting by Hirschten

VICTOR FRANKL

Audience: Adults

After surviving internment in a Nazi concentration camp during World War II, Victor Frankl wrote the book *"Man's Search for Meaning."* In it he shared many stories about how having a love and a purpose in life can help people persevere through such horrors.

One of the stories he wrote was of a woman who was

dying. Frankl was caring for her in her sickness. He noticed that she seemed happy and content despite being so ill under miserable circumstances. He asked her why she was happy. She stated that she had been so spoiled in her former life that she was thankful now to gain a new perspective. Pointing to a tree outside her window that had two chestnut blossoms she said that it was the only friend she had. She said that she talked to the tree to free her from loneliness.

Hearing this made Frankl worry that she was becoming delirious with her sickness. He asked her if the tree said anything back to her. She replied, "Yes, it said to me, 'I am here, I am here-- I am life, eternal life.'"

A few days later, the woman died. Victor Frankl lived for another fifty-two years working as an influential psychiatrist and writer. Throughout his writings, he spread the positive message that all people can find meaning and purpose in their existence.

Thoughts: In our darkest moments symbols can open our eyes to larger truths. Life always persists, pushing its way through the cracks in the pavement. Viewing these small miracles can awaken us to having a thankful heart. As artists we can use these symbols to communicate what it is that we are so desperately trying to say.

Source: This is a true story found in Victor Frankl's book *"Man's Search for Meaning."*

Classroom Ideas: Ask the students if they have any symbols in their own lives that help remind them of larger truths. Would the symbol be recognized by others or is it personal? How can they best use the symbol to communicate through their artwork?

****

*"The artist has to be something like a whale
swimming with his mouth open,
absorbing everything
until he has what he really needs."
-Romare Bearden*

****

"Give and Take" Painting by Hirschten

THE FISHERMAN AND HIS MUSIC

Audience: All Ages

Once upon a time there was a fisherman who preferred playing his flute to catching fish. One day he devised a plan to play his music and catch fish at the same time. Placing his net on the shore of the lake, he tried to lure the fish to the net with his most elegant playing. He hoped that they would jump out of the water and into his net that was lying on the ground.

After a while he gave up. No fish had fallen for his trick. Throwing his net into the water he pulled the line in. Much to his surprise, he found that there was a whole school of fish hovering right below the water before him. They had come to listen to his music! Now the fisherman's task was easy.

Thoughts: Aesop, the writer of this story, stated that the moral of the tale is "Good fortune happens when you least expect it." While this is true, I'd like to add another moral to the tale especially for artists. Others will be lured into the beauty of what you do if you love it; cast your net by asking for their support. They may be listening to you just under the surface of the water.

Source: Written by the Greek author Aesop circa 600BC.

Classroom Ideas: Ask the class, "What is your favorite

thing to do? Are there ways of incorporating it into your least favorite tasks?" For example if you love listening to music but hate washing dishes, listen to music while you wash dishes. Or if you hate being at work but love your family, put up pictures of them on your desk at work to get you through your day.

****

"All instruction is but a finger pointing to the moon; and those whose gaze is fixed upon the finger will never see beyond."
-Buddha

****

"Peonies in a Cut Glass Vase" Painting by Hirschten

THE WORKS OF THE LOUVRE

Audience: All Ages

In 1939 Germany invaded Poland. In response France and Britain declared war on Germany. Fearing that bombs might be dropped in an attack on Paris, the curators of the Louvre museum took action. The museum held many of the world's priceless works of art. Paintings by Rembrandt and Rubens as well as many sculptures from ancient Greece were housed in the old royal palace, the Louvre. The curators boxed up 3690 items from the museum's collection. These works of art were then shipped out of Paris to various remote countryside locations.

Over the next few years, this collection of art traveled throughout France in the hopes of evading being seized by the German army. This tremendous feat was successful. When the war ended in 1945 every single one of the 3690 items were returned to the Louvre museum.

Thoughts: The amazing aspect of this story is how the people of France valued their national art collection so highly they made it a top priority to get it out of harm's way during World War II. This was at great personal risk to the museum curators and civilians who aided the project. It shows that works of art are incredibly valuable to civilization. This was an act of gratitude.

Source: This is a true story. Read "*Saving Mona Lisa: The Battle to Protect the Louvre and its Treasures During World War II*" for an exciting in-depth telling of this story.

Classroom Ideas: Ask your students what they would grab out of their homes if their house was on fire. With both adults and children alike you will get interesting answers. The answer to this question shows a lot about a person and what he or she values. Asking this question can also help people to figure out what direction to go when creating future art projects. If they would grab a photo album of their family maybe their next project should involve portraits of their family members.

****

"It is the artist's business to make sunshine when the sun fails."
-Romain Rolland

****

"The End of the Stream" Painting by Hirschten

THOREAU ON WALDEN POND

Audience: All Ages

Between 1845 and 1847 Henry David Thoreau went to live in a small cabin on Walden Pond in Concord, Massachusetts. He wanted to get away from the restrictions of society, be independent, and live closer to nature. For two years, two months and two days Thoreau successfully lived his dream of being a hermit in the woods. During that time he thought a lot about humanity's relationship with and dependence on nature. He decided that he wanted to learn to be happy anywhere regardless of his circumstances. "I would rather sit on a pumpkin and have it all to myself," he said, "than be crowded on a velvet cushion." He believed that people who look for bad things will find bad things "even in paradise."

Thoreau wrote a book about his experience called "*Walden, Or Life in the Woods.*" In it he urged people to "carve and paint the very atmosphere through which we look," to create the world we want to see by becoming an active participant in the process of nature. The book is now famous and has influenced many people.

Thoughts: It is easy to get caught up in the entrapments of our everyday lives. Sometimes we feel powerless to change them. Yet every choice you have made up until now has put you where you are today. If you don't care for your surroundings, make plans to change them. Only you have that power.

Source: This is a true story. Read the book written by Thoreau, "*Walden, Or Life in the Woods*," first published in 1854.

Classroom Ideas: Go out into the woods for a meditative class project. Ask the students to sit in silence, listening only to the sound of nature. (Thoreau loved his solitude!) They can write or illustrate their experience. Ask them to share what they observed when you return to the classroom.

****

"I learned this, at least, by my experiment; that if one advances confidently in the direction of his dreams, and endeavors to live the life which he has imagined, he will meet with a success unexpected in common hours."
-Thoreau

****

PART 5

SHARING

"Doll from India" Illustration by Hirschten

THE THREE DOLLS

Audience: All Ages

Once upon a time there was a king who loved riddles. He sent a message out to all of his people asking them to send him riddles so that he could try to solve them. Many people sent these puzzles to the king and usually he could figure them out in an instant because he was very clever.

One day the king received a strange package. He opened the gift and inside he found three dolls. They were elegantly dressed in silk robes. They each had jet black, real human hair woven onto their heads. They each had the same carved noses and chins. In fact the three dolls looked exactly alike. At the bottom of the box there was a piece of paper. It read, "These three dolls may look alike, but they are very different. The riddle is: how are they different?"

The king looked at the dolls again. He could find no scratch or mark to distinguish the dolls from one another. He could not figure out the answer to this riddle.

After sitting and thinking for some time the king called in one of his wise advisors. He told the wise man the riddle and showed him the dolls. The wise man walked around and around the dolls twisting his beard as he thought. The wise man circled and circled the dolls saying nothing for hours. Finally the king said, "Stop! That is enough, you may leave."

Sad that the wise man could not solve the riddle, the king sat down on his throne to think again. Suddenly he jumped up. "Fools rush in where wise men fear to tread. If a wise man could not answer the riddle I should ask a fool."

So a fool was brought to the castle. The king told the fool

the riddle and showed him the dolls. The fool picked up the dolls and started juggling them in the air. "Dollies-- ha ha!" he shouted. After only a minute of this, the king said, "Stop! That is enough, you may leave."

Sad that the fool could not solve the riddle, the king hung his head to think some more. Then he thought of the artist. The artist lived in the village, where he would paint murals on the houses and bend wood into sculptures. He would share stories with the children and play his flute in the mornings. Sometimes the artist seemed very wise to the king and other times he seemed to be a fool. The king called for his guards to bring the artist to him.

As soon as the artist arrived, the king told him the riddle and showed him the dolls. The artist studied the dolls, then said, "I have found that the inside of a person can be very different from the outside. And I can get to the inside through either their eyes or their ears. We can't get inside the eyes of these dolls, but I think we can get in the ears." The king nodded his head in agreement.

The artist pulled three strands of hair from his head. Taking one hair he poked it through the ear of the first doll. The hair went into the brain of the doll and wound itself into a nest. "Ahh," said the artist. "This doll is a wise one for she has taken something in and held it."

The artist then poked the second hair into the ear of the next doll. It went into the brain and then came out the other ear. The hair fell to the table. "This doll is a fool," declared the artist. "For what she has heard went in one ear and out the other."

The artist picked up the last strand of hair and pushed it into the ear of the third doll. The hair twisted around the brain and then came out of the mouth. "This doll is an artist," he said. "For what she has heard she has chosen to share with others."

The king smiled and said, "I believe that you have solved the riddle. Thank you."

Thoughts: The instinct to share our joys, hopes, dreams, and injustices drives many artists. The best work shares common elements of the human experience and can be labeled as having a "classic," timeless quality. When these common elements or archetypes are expressed through art, the work resonates a chord in the viewer. Regardless of background, age, or time period, a person can look at a work and see themselves in it. The work will be successful because it has voiced a universal truth. The work will be successful because the artist has had the courage to be honest.

Source: This is a folktale originally from India and was adapted by the storyteller David Novak for the book, "*Ready-To-Tell Tales*." I have altered it further still.

Classroom Ideas: Bring dolls of various types into class and have the students draw the "inner world" of the character. The thoughts and feelings the students imagine the characters to have can be mapped out onto the body image. This can also be paired with body mapping exercises used in art therapy. Very moving body mapping art has been created by HIV/AIDS patients in a project developed by Colin Ameleh at the University of Cape Town.

****

"One purpose of art is to alert people to things they might have missed."
-Corita Kent

****

"You Are My Sunshine" Painting by Hirschten

THE RAINBOW

Audience: All Ages

One day I was walking to meet my daughter at the bus stop. Rain was blowing in my face and I was squinting against the shining sun.

Suddenly I remembered something my step-dad had told me years before. When there is sun coming at an angle and rain at the same time, there is ALWAYS a rainbow. You just have to turn away from the sun to see the light shining into the rain.

I turned around and there was a fully arched rainbow! It seemed that one end of it started at my house.

I stood for a moment smiling at this happy site, when a man in a car drove past. I pointed urgently behind him and mouthed, "Rainbow!" I'm not sure if he understood or thought I was crazy.

Later I realized that it was the artist in me that wanted so desperately to share that beautiful miraculous moment with a complete stranger. For that is what art is all about: sharing.

Thoughts: There are many different reasons why people come to artwork. My own reasons have changed drastically over the years. Yet from art therapy to realism, what all art has in common is that it is communicating something from the artist to the viewer. Much of art, especially landscape work, is intended to share the beauty of nature with the viewer.

Source: This is a personal story by the author.

Classroom Ideas: Prompt the students to answer the question of what ideas they are trying to share through the medium of their artwork. Children can be asked to depict their favorite things that they wish to share with their family members.

****

"The artist has so much love to give back to the universe that it spills over, and the fallen drops become 'works of art.'
It is love in another form."
-Nancy Jackson

****

"My Daughter" Painting by Hirschten

THE MAMA CAT

Audience: All Ages

Once upon a time there was a Mama Cat who was lying peacefully on her front porch basking in the sunshine. She yawned, stretched, and looked down at her three little baby kittens. She licked their faces and all was right with the world.

Suddenly a large dog came bounding into the yard. He barked loudly at the cats in his gruff voice. The Mama Cat stood up and said something to the dog that made him turn tail, walking calmly out of the yard. Can you guess what the Mama Cat said?

She said, "Bark, bark, bark, bark, bark!" After the dog was gone she turned to her baby kittens and said, "You see, my dears, this is why it is so helpful to learn a second language."

Thoughts: Art is another form of language. One of the main purposes of art is to communicate with the viewer. Even within the art world we speak different art languages according to our styles and intent. Sometimes there are issues that are more easily communicated visually or musically than with spoken word. Sometimes victims of trauma can start their healing process with art. Art gives voice to many people who would not have the courage to express themselves otherwise.

Source: This is a folktale from Wales. Years ago I heard a Welsh storyteller, Esyllt Harker, share it in both English and Welsh.

Classroom Ideas: Challenge your students to define what they are trying to say with their artwork. Why did they choose this medium to communicate it?

****

"Creativity serves to bring some of our hidden life into expression in order that we might come to see who we are."
-John O'Donohue

****

"The Ghost Nun" Illustration by Hirschten

THE GHOST NUN

Audience: Age 8 and up

Once upon a time a group of Catholics settled in the frontier of Indiana and built a school. With time, many young people came there to learn. One teacher in the school was a nun who loved to paint. She painted pictures of the farmland around the school and the flowers in the garden.

Everyone thought her paintings were beautiful. She was asked by the head of the school to teach art classes. So the nun set up a classroom as an art studio and started teaching art.

Soon the nun was asked to paint portraits of the other teachers in the school. One by one the nun painted the pictures and hung them on the wall of the great hall. Again everyone praised her for her talent as an artist. Finally the nun had painted every teacher in the school except herself.

Alone in the studio she began her self-portrait by propping a mirror in front of her canvas. First she drew the outline of her form. Then she started painting the background of the room and the black and white cloth of her nun's robes. The sun was setting outside, changing the light in the room to an orange glow. She had finished all of the painting except for her face. The nun cleaned her brushes and left the studio to eat dinner.

In the dining hall the nun was asked by another teacher what she had worked on that day. The nun whispered to the teacher, "I have almost finished my self-portrait and I think it will be my best painting yet!" "That is wonderful," said the other teacher. "Our set of portraits for the great hall will be complete!"

The next day, however, when the morning light hit the nun's face she did not wake up. She was sick with a fever. She could not eat or drink. After several days of pain the nun died.

When the funeral was over her fellow teachers went to clean out the art studio. There was no one else who could teach art. When they opened the door they found a nun sitting in front of the unfinished portrait, crying. They walked toward the crying nun to comfort her, but when she turned toward them they were horrified to see that where the face should be was a black hole. This ghost had no face, just like the painting behind it. The teachers ran from the room, locking the door behind them.

No one was brave enough to enter the room again. After a few years the building was torn down and replaced with another. But it is said that the ghost nun still haunts the grounds of the school, crying over the unfinished painting.

Thoughts: Each of us has a calling or "life's work" that festers at the back of our mind waiting for us to complete it. The story of the ghost nun reminds us that the most tragic outcome would be to not finish your life's work. Many artists know what their life's work is but they don't have the courage to complete or even start it. If this is the case for you, I urge you to pick up the paint brush, pencil, or whatever your instrument of choice is and complete your calling.

Source: This is an Indiana ghost story. It is part of the folkloric tradition of St. Mary of the Woods College near Terre Haute, Indiana.

Classroom Ideas: Ask the students to brainstorm and write down what their "life's work" is. Share the ideas out loud and formulate plans to make the ideas come to fruition. Another twist on this question is to ask what is the purpose they are trying to express as artists. Is there a point at which their work will be completed?

****

"Art is like a bright star up ahead in the darkness of the world. It can lead peoples through the darkness. Art is a guide for every person who is looking for something."
-Thornton Dial

****

"Measure for Measure" Painting by Hirschten

SAINT VALENTINE

Audience: Age 8 and up

Historians know little about how true the stories of Saint Valentine are. According to legend he was a third century Christian Bishop who lived in Rome. Against the wishes of the Roman government, he married couples. Because of this he was sentenced to death. While he was waiting to be executed he was given one last request by his jailers. He asked for a sheet of paper. On that sheet of paper he wrote a letter expressing his love for family and friends. The date of his execution was February 14th.

Now every February 14th we celebrate Valentine's Day. It is a day when we write and create cards that express our love for family and friends.

Thoughts: Sometimes all that is needed to inspire art is a little sugar. Love can be the fountain from which our passion grows.

Source: There is no primary documentation on the life of Saint Valentine. This story is therefore a hodgepodge of legend.

Classroom Ideas: Create Valentine's Day cards for loved ones.

****

"No man is an island, entire of itself."
-John Donne

****

"Gunnywolf" Illustration by Hirschten

THE GUNNYWOLF

Audience: All Ages

Once upon a time there was a little girl who lived in a cottage at the edge of the woods with her mother. One day her mother asked her if she would like to go to the market. The girl said that she would rather stay home. The mother was not sure this was a good idea because the girl was still quite young, but she agreed to let her stay. Before leaving the mother made the girl promise that she would not go into the woods while she was gone because a Gunnywolf lived there.

As the mother walked down the road toward the market, the girl waved goodbye to her. She sat on the front step of her house enjoying the warm sun on her face. She listed to the birds singing up in the trees and started singing a song to herself. It went "Kum-kwah- kee-wah. Kum-kwah- kee-wahaha."

Suddenly the girl stood up. She saw white wildflowers in bloom across the field. She thought it would be wonderful to make a bouquet for her mother as a surprise gift. She crossed the field and started picking the flowers, all the while singing her song, "Kum-kwah- kee-wah. Kum-kwah- kee-wahaha."

When she had picked all of the white flowers, the girl was very excited to see pink flowers growing by the fence. She thought the pink flowers would look wonderful next to the white. As she added them to her bouquet she sang her song, "Kum-kwah- kee-wah. Kum-kwah- kee-wahaha."

The little girl spotted purple flowers in the shade of the trees. Purple was her mother's favorite color! She ran over to the purple flowers and started picking them. She sang her song happily, "Kum-kwah- kee-wah. Kum-kwah- kee-wahaha."

Suddenly, the Gunnywolf jumped up. He growled at the girl and said, "Little girl, sing that good sweet song again." She trembled and shook as she sang, "Kum-kwah- kee-wah. Kum-kwah- kee-wahaha. Kum-kwah- kee-wah. Kum-kwah-kee-wahaha."

As she sang the wolf nodded his head, lay down on the ground, and went to sleep. He snored loudly as the little girl tried to make her getaway. "Pitty- pat- pitty- pat- pitty- pat-pit. Pitty- pat- pitty- pat- pitty- pat- pit," went her feet on the ground.

Up jumped the Gunnywolf. He ran after her, "hunkacha-hunkacha- hunkacha- hunckacha." He growled at the girl and said, "Little girl, sing that good sweet song again." Afraid to look in his face, she sang to him, "Kum-kwah- kee-wah. Kum-kwah- kee-wahaha. Kum-kwah- kee-wah. Kum-kwah-kee-wahaha."

As she sang the wolf nodded his head, lay down on the ground, and went to sleep. He snored loudly as the little girl tried to make her getaway. "Pitty- pat- pitty- pat- pitty- pat-pit. Pitty- pat- pitty- pat- pitty- pat- pit," went her feet on the ground.

Up jumped the Gunnywolf. He ran after her, "hunkacha-hunkacha- hunkacha- hunkacha." He growled at the girl and said, "Little girl, sing that good sweet song again." More confidently this time she sang, "Kum-kwah- kee-wah. Kum-kwah- kee-wahaha. Kum-kwah- kee-wah. Kum-kwah- kee-wahaha."

As she sang the wolf nodded his head, lay down on the ground, and went to sleep. He snored loudly as the little girl tiptoed away. "Pitty- pat- pitty- pat- pitty- pat- pit. Pitty- pat-pitty- pat- pitty- pat- pit," softly went her feet until she reached the door to her house. She slammed it shut behind her and breathed a sigh of relief. Never again was she afraid of the wolf, however, because she had learned that music can tame even the most savage of beasts.

Thoughts: We all have metaphorical monsters to battle as we go through our daily lives. Often art can tame those beasts when other forms of communication have broken down. Art can be used to make political statements or to show others how their "beastly" actions make us feel.

Source: This folktale is of African American origin. It is often attributed to Wilhelmina Harper who first documented it in 1918. There is speculation as to whether the song sung by the little girls and the term "Gunnywolf" may be derived from African words, but this has not been proven.

Classroom Ideas: Young children love when this story is told with puppets. For them it functions as a more empowering "Little Red Riding Hood" story. Adults are more likely to connect the metaphor of the beast to enemies in their own lives. Have adults think of a time they had trouble communicating with someone and brainstorm ways to express their feeling with art.

****

"The pen is mightier than the sword."
-Ahiqar

****

PART 6

PERSERVERANCE

"Black Cat" Painting by Hishida Shunso Circa 1910

THE BOY WHO DREW CATS

Audience: Age 8 and up

Once upon a time there was a boy who loved nothing more in the world than to draw cats. He was the youngest son in his poor family. His parents saw that he didn't like farming so they decided to send him away to a temple. There he would study to become a priest.

Yet when the boy arrived at the temple the elders were not pleased that he wanted to draw cats all the time. His elders saw that he didn't like being a priest. They decided to send him away.

Not sure where to go, the boy wandered the land for many days. Finally, he arrived at an abandoned temple. Not only was the temple a perfect shelter for the boy but it had paper screen walls. The boy could create a mural full of his favorite creature, cats! He set to work until he had covered the walls with every type of cat. They were fluffy, fat and thin, striped and solid. They were sleeping and playing, pouncing and eating. Yawning, the boy put down his brush. He explored the temple looking for a place to sleep. Finding a cupboard filled with linens, he nestled down in it and closed the door.

In the middle of the night the boy was awakened by the sound of howling, hissing and shrieking. Scared, the boy stayed hidden in the cupboard until the sounds subsided.

In the morning the boy tentatively opened the door. Right away he saw that the cats he had drawn were not in their original positions! They had moved all about and some of them had blood on their mouths. Now they were still again as the boy tiptoed through the temple.

In the main hall the boy found the dead body of the

Goblin Rat. The boy realized that this must be the legendary temple haunted by the Goblin Rat. The Goblin Rat would come out at night and eat any visitors to the temple. But now the cat drawings had magically defeated him!

The boy ran back to his village to share the news that the Goblin Rat was defeated. The boy was hailed as a hero. The priests gave him the old haunted temple as his new home. People traveled from far and wide to see the magical mural of cats.

Thoughts: Many people struggle to find a profession that will suit them. This can be especially hard for creative souls. Keep searching, keep doing what you love, and everything will fall into place.

Source: This is a Japanese folktale.

Classroom Ideas: Since cats do not sit readily for portraits, take cat photos and do a study on drawing this magnificent animal.

****

"While in the process of creating anything in our lives, we continue to create ourselves... We are the canvas, the poem, the song... the unfinished masterpiece!"
-Joy Wallace

****

"Reincarnation" Painting by Hirschten

MATISSE'S SECOND LIFE

Audience: All Ages

Henri Matisse was a respected French painter known for his bright vivid colors. In 1941 he had surgery for cancer that weakened his body. It caused him to need to use a wheelchair. He was unable to stand at his easel to paint.

Matisse sent a letter to his ex-wife to make peace with her. He set his projects to rest thinking that the end of his life was near. But then an extraordinary thing happened. Matisse's energy renewed. He switched from painting to creating cut paper collages. He made many colorful, dynamic designs of all different shapes and sizes. He had the cut pieces put on a wall to rearrange them over and over again until he finalized the design and had it glued to a backing. He illustrated and wrote a book called "*Jazz*" about improvisational jazz music and "being at one with the audience." Matisse called this time period of renewal "Une Seconde Vie [A Second Life]."

He lived for another fourteen years and produced an exciting body of work that became even more famous than his original paintings.

Thoughts: The end of one time period means the beginning of another. Always look for ways to express yourself even if your former instrument has been taken away. It may turn out to be an even better fit for you than the one you had before!

Source: This is a true story. Read "*Henri Matisse: A Second Life*" by Alastair Sooke for further details on this story.

Classroom Ideas: Bring glue, scissors and colorful paper to make collages inspired by Matisse's work.

****

"Only what I created after my illness constitutes my real self; free, liberated."
-Henri Matisse

****

"Skulls" Painting by Hirschten

JACK AND THE GHOST

Audience: Age 8 and up

Once upon a time there was a boy named Jack. He lived on a farm with his mother. A drought swept over the land. It didn't rain for months. None of the crops that Jack and his mother had planted in the ground grew. Jack looked at their supply of food. It wouldn't last them through the winter. "Mother," he said, "I know you think I am young but now is the time for me to go seek my fortune. If I don't do something now, we will starve to death."

Jack's mother hung her head. "You are right my son. I'll let you go. But first let me make you a sack of food to take with you."

Soon Jack was walking down the road with a sack of bread and soup on his back. Jack walked up the hills and down the dales. The sun rose in the sky then sank down again. As the sky got dark Jack came to a town. He knocked on the door of an inn. The innkeeper answered the door. "Please," Jack asked, "I am seeking my fortune. Do you have a job you can give me? I'll clean dishes, mop the floors... I'll do anything." "Well now," said the innkeeper, "you'll never make a fortune washing dishes. Are you a brave boy?" "Oh yes sir, I'm brave," said Jack quickly. "Do you see that house up on the hill behind you?" asked the innkeeper.

Jack looked behind him. An iron fence surrounded a yard filled with ripe apple trees. A path led to an old mansion. It had turrets and carved wood trim. Many of the windows were broken. The house looked dark and forlorn as if no one had lived there in years.

"Yes, I see that house," said Jack. The innkeeper leaned closer to Jack and whispered, "It is said that the house is haunted. No one has been brave enough to stay there overnight. If you can stay there for one night the house is yours." Jack gasped, "The whole house, really!?"

Jack looked back at the mansion. The fruit on the apple trees alone was worth a lot in the market. He and his mother would be set for the winter. "I'll try it," said Jack. "Well, good luck to you, my boy," said the innkeeper. "You will need it."

Jack started off for the house. Leaves crunched under his step. The heavy gate creaked as he opened it. An owl hooted up in the tree. "Oh now, you don't scare me," said Jack as he mounted the steps to the front porch. Knocking on the door Jack called out, "Hello, is anybody home?" He was met with silence. The door opened easily for him as he gently turned the knob. To his left was an art studio. Cobwebs covered an old easel. To his right was a formal dining room. The crystal chandelier swayed slightly as wind whipped through the house. As Jack shut the door behind him his stomach rumbled. He had eaten all of the bread on his long journey but he still had a jar of soup. Deciding that he would find the kitchen to heat up his food, Jack followed his nose past the dining room into a large old-fashioned kitchen. It had a stone fireplace with a cauldron hanging from a hook. There was wood for a fire. Jack arranged the logs and lit the fire. Soon it was blazing. He poured the soup into the cauldron and sat back to watch it bubble. That was when he heard the first sound.

Something bumped up inside the chimney. "Look out below... I'm falling," cried a voice. Down from the shaft of the chimney fell a pair of legs with no body. They bounced out of the fire then ran around the room. Around and around they ran in circles. Jack's eyes popped out of his face. He held his breath. "Stop it!" screamed Jack at the top of his lungs. To his surprise the legs stopped and turned to face him. "Uhhh... you go sit down in that chair," commanded Jack. The legs walked calmly to the chair, sat down and started rocking back and forth. "Well that was weird," thought Jack. His stomach grumbled again. He turned to stir his soup. As he leaned over the fire, he heard the second sound.

Something bumped up inside the chimney. "Look out below... I'm falling," cried a voice. Down from the shaft of the chimney fell a torso and arms. They bounced out of the fire and flew around the room. Around and around they flew in circles. Jack's eyes popped out of his face. He held his breath. "Stop it!" screamed Jack at the top of his lungs. The torso and arms stopped and turned to face him. "Uhhh... you go attach yourself to your legs," commanded Jack. The torso floated to the legs, attached themselves and the body started rocking back and forth. "Well this just gets weirder and weirder," thought Jack. "But nothing bad has happened." His stomach grumbled again. He turned to stir his soup. As he leaned over the fire, he heard the third sound.

Something bumped up inside the chimney. "Look out below... I'm falling," cried a voice. Down from the shaft of the chimney fell a head. It fell in the pot of soup. It bounced out and bopped around the room. It hit the ceiling and the wall, then the floor. It bounced like a wild basketball. Around and around it bounced. Jack's eyes popped out of his face. He held his breath. "Stop it!" screamed Jack at the top of his lungs. The head stopped and turned to face him. "Uhhh... you go attach yourself to your body," commanded Jack. The head floated to the body, attached itself and the entire apparition stood.

Jack bit his fingernails. "Jack," said the ghost, "I must thank you. No one has ever stayed long enough for me to put myself back together. For this I have a reward for you. Follow me."

The ghost crossed the room. He opened a small door leading downstairs to a cellar. The ghost pointed to a spot on the dirt floor. "This is where I buried my treasure. When I was young I traveled around the world to paint. I gathered a trove of valuable sculptures, carvings and jewelry in exchange for my work. I was murdered years ago by someone who wanted to steal my treasure, but he never found it. The treasure is yours now, Jack. Now I will rest in peace... and not in pieces." With a gust of wind the apparition dissipated into thin air.

Jack ran to find a shovel. He dug and dug at the spot until he hit a solid box. Opening it, Jack found a dazzling assortment of treasures. He and his mother would be set for life!

The next day Jack fetched his mother. They fixed up the mansion on the hill and lived there happily for the rest of their days.

Thoughts: Oftentimes people, especially artists, let their fears get in the way of achieving their goals. We must persevere in every endeavor of our lives if we are to get to the rich reward of a job well done.

Source: This is a folktale of British origin popular in the Appalachian region of the United States.

Classroom Ideas: After reading this story ask the students what they would imagine being in the box of treasure. What would they have to do to make a treasure?

****

"If you hold your hand in the flame long
enough a flower will blossom."
-Pablo Neruda

****

"Impression, Sunrise" Painting by Monet

IMPRESSIONISM

Audience: All Ages

In France, during the nineteenth century, the Academie des Beaux-Arts would host an annual "Salon de Paris" exhibition. This was a prestigious show of the "best" new artwork created by French artists. The show was supported by the government. It was considered essential for every professional artist to take part in the "Salon de Paris" or they were not favored by art buyers.

In 1863, however, there were so many works rejected

from the exhibit for being too innovative there was an outcry from the art community. They accused the Academie of only exhibiting an old-fashioned style and being unwilling to display new works. The Emperor Napoleon III was brought in to view the rejected works. He declared that they would have a second exhibit that year. In it they would show only the work that was rejected by the committee. They dubbed this exhibit the "Salon de Refuses."

The members of the Academie thought that the exhibit of rejected work would prove to the world how terrible it was and how superior the Academie's selections were. This was not the case, however. Not all, but many people loved the "Salon de Refuses" works. Far more people visited the new exhibit than the old.

A few years later a group of artists formed. Many of them had been part of the "Salon de Refuses." At first they called themselves the "Anonymous Society of Painters, Sculptors, and Engravers." This name changed, however, after the first exhibit. A critic by the name of Louis Leroy insulted a painting created by Monet for the show. The painting was called "Impression, Sunrise." In it Monet was focused on capturing the light and atmosphere of a harbor in the early morning sunrise. The critic did not like it and stated

"Impression, I was certain of it. I was just telling myself that since I was impressed, there must be some impression in it... and what freedom, what ease of workmanship! Wallpaper in its embryonic state is more finished than that seascape." Yet other people loved how Monet had let go of the unimportant details of his sunrise scene.

Eventually, the group embraced the term "Impressionism," making it the word to describe their new popular art movement.

Thoughts: Just as life is always growing and changing, so too do art movements. Innovation is essential for growth and should never be suppressed. While it is fine for selectors of any given art show to pick their favorites, this only shows us one thing: what the selectors like. It does not necessarily reflect the vision or message that the public is craving to hear. Create artwork that speaks to you. The audience that is yearning for that message will embrace it.

Source: This is a true story. There are numerous books on the subject including "*Impressionism: Origins, Practice,*

Reception" by Belinda Thomson.

Classroom Ideas: Mimic the Impressionist painters by picking a spot outside to paint. Go there several times with your class to paint the scene. Focus on attempting to reflect the atmosphere and light of the place. Notice how every day is different, how no two leaves are the same.

****

"The only constant is change.
You cannot step twice into the same river."
-Heraclitus

****

"An Explosion" Painting by Hirschten

THE MUSICIAN, ORPHEUS

Audience: Age 8 and up

In the land of ancient Greece a son was born to Euterpe, the muse of joy and delight. She gave her son, Orpheus, the gift of musical talent. He could charm any creature when he sang.   Apollo, the god of light, gave him a harp to complement his singing. If people argued, Orpheus could sooth them to sleep with his music. If he strolled down a path while playing a tune, stones and trees would sway to the rhythm of his song. Streams and rivers would alter their path to be closer to him. Not surprisingly, women flocked to worship Orpheus, wishing to be his bride.

Orpheus had already chosen a wife, however, when he came of age. Eurydice was a woman he had known since childhood. She did not worship him but understood the language of his song. They were married and briefly enjoyed the comfort of each other's company.

One day disaster struck when the couple went for a walk on a mountain path. Eurydice accidentally stepped on a snake that was sleeping in the tall grass. It bit her with a poisonous venom. She died instantly. Orpheus was devastated. He cried out with hauntingly painful music. Zeus, king of the gods, heard his cry. He allowed Orpheus to enter the underworld to convince Hades, god of death, to bring his wife back to life.

As Orpheus entered the first chamber of hell, the three-headed guard dog, Cerberus, leaped upon him. Orpheus quickly sang a melody to calm the beast. The dog fell into a trance. Orpheus descended down the steep narrow path until he reached the throne room of Hades, where he pleaded for his wife to be returned by singing of his sorrow.

Hades became tearful and agreed to allow Orpheus to

return Eurydice to the world of the living under one condition. Orpheus must ascend up the stairs of hell with Eurydice walking behind him. He must trust that she is following him and not look back to see her until they reach the land above. Orpheus happily agreed. Together he and his wife began the long climb upward.

With the haunting sounds of hell echoing the in chamber, Orpheus could not hear the footsteps of Eurydice. He began to doubt the promise Hades had made. He began to doubt that Eurydice was behind him. Suddenly he could bear it no longer; Orpheus turned back. He saw Eurydice's face for only a brief moment. She was then hurled back into the pits of hell as he was banished to the world above.

Orpheus lamented the loss of his wife for the rest of his life. Never again was he able to sing of joy.

Thoughts: Hidden between the lines of the story of Orpheus is a message of perseverance. Our main character came very close to defeating death with the artistry of his music. He failed, however, when he succumbed to doubt. Never give up. Never stop moving forward. There is light at the end of the tunnel if you have the patience to reach it.

Source: This is an ancient Greek myth. Versions of it were written down by Apollonius of Rhodes, Virgil, and Ovid.

Classroom Ideas: Ask the students to draw depictions of what they would do to charm Hades. Once they are finished ask them if these ideas would charm their friends and family. If so, what steps would they have to take to make it happen? What obstacles would they need to overcome to reach their goal?

****

"To everything there is a season, and a time to every purpose under heaven."
-Ecclesiastes 3:1

****

Thomas Edison in his Workshop Circa 1880

THE LIGHT BULB

Audience: All Ages

When Thomas Edison assembled a team of engineers in Menlo Park, New Jersey, in 1876 he created an "Invention Factory." Far away from the distractions found in the cities of New York and Philadelphia, he placed in his factory a library, office space, a machine building center, and a scientific laboratory.

Edison worked long hours in the factory. He often

worked sixteen hour days, attributing his success to not having a clock in his workspace. He and his team patented many inventions during that time including the phonograph, a new telephone, a motion picture camera, batteries, and the electric light bulb.

Another version of the light bulb had already been invented. But it was not very bright. No one wanted to use it in their homes. Edison wanted to create a bulb that was safe, affordable, and emitted a soft gentle light. He worked tirelessly, filling 40,000 pages worth of notes on the project. Finally he was able to design a light bulb that could stay on continuously for forty hours. The secret ingredient was carbonized bamboo.

The light bulb needed entire electrical systems to be connected to people's homes. This system took off, becoming a popular and efficient means of supplying electric energy around the world.

Thoughts: The lesson to be learned from Edison's story is the importance of perseverance. If something isn't quite right, like the original electric bulb, it can always be improved upon.

Source: This is a true story. Children will enjoy the nonfiction graphic novel, *"Thomas Edison and the Lightbulb"* by Scott Welvaert.

Classroom Ideas: Children love brainstorming ideas for inventions. Ask them to design and illustrate one new idea. (You may have to discourage them from talking during that time or you will end up with twenty-five inventions for windshield wiper glasses!) Adults can be prompted to share their own stories of perseverance.

****

"The greatest gift is a portion of thyself."
-Emerson

****

"Tree on a Summer Evening" Painting by Hirschten

HUNDERTWASSER

Audience: Ages 10 and up

In 1928 Friedensreich Stowasser was born in Vienna, Austria. His mother was Jewish and his father was Catholic. During World War II Friedensreich and his mother lived in fear that the Nazis would discover their Jewish heritage. After seeing the geometric marching formations of the Nazi soldiers, Friedensreich grew to detest the straight line. To him the straight line represented oppressive totalitarian governments. When he later became a painter and architect he incorporated organic flowing lines into his work instead.

Friedensreich wanted to encourage people's lives to be

free from oppression and more in sync with nature. When he designed buildings he used no straight lines and put trees on the rooftops. He felt that if trees had to be torn down to build a building, people should replace them on the tops of buildings because the closer humans are to nature the closer they are to their true selves. He wanted for buildings to fit the human body and cater to its needs.

Friedensreich changed his name several times. He became most well-known under the name "Hundertwasser," which means one hundred waters. He also went by the names "Renentag," which means rainy day, and "Dunkelbunt," which means darkly multi-colored.

Thoughts: Hundertwasser is best known for turning things upside down in a revolutionary way. He brought a breath of fresh air to the world of architecture. He wasn't afraid of changing his name, splashing bright paint everywhere and even taking his clothes off in public! Sometimes when someone has experienced extreme oppression and seen the horrible consequences of it he or she can open our eyes to new ways of seeing the world, changing it for the better.

Source: This is a true story. Read *"Hundertwasser"* by Harry Rand.

Classroom Ideas: For painting projects students can create designs using no straight lines but spirals and circles inspired by Hundertwasser's work. I've also done an architecture lesson with children where we redesigned our elementary school. The school had no playground because it is in the inner city of Indianapolis, so many of the students added playground equipment to their designs. Imagine our delight when the next year the school was renovated to include a playground on the roof! Hundertwasser would have been proud.

****

"When we dream alone, it is only a dream but when many dream together it is the beginning of a new reality."
-Hundertwasser

****

PART 7

DEFINING SUCCESS

"Sunflowers in the Light" Painting by Hirschten

THE $20 BILL

Audience: All Ages

Once upon a time in New Jersey a man walked into a grocery store. He selected his items and went to pay for them at the cash register. He placed a $20 bill on the counter so the clerk could give him his change.

There was a puddle of water on the counter and the $20 bill sat in it for a moment. When the clerk picked it up she

189

found that ink came off the bill and bled onto her fingers. As the man left the store she wondered if the money was fake. But the pictures on it were perfect and she knew this man. His name was Emanuel Ninger. He and his family were well-respected in the community. It didn't seem possible that he would give her a fake bill.

But the year was 1896 and $20 was a lot of money then. She took the bill to the bank. They looked at it under a magnifying glass and confirmed that it was a fake bill.

The police were called in to investigate. They went to the home of Emanuel Ninger. In his attic they found an art studio. On one side of the room were three large floral paintings. They were skillfully rendered. On the other side there was a desk. On that desk was a half-painted $20 bill.

Ninger was arrested and sent to jail for several years. The police took the three paintings from his home to pay for expenses. The paintings were sold in an auction for more than $5,000 each.

It had taken Emanuel Ninger the same amount of time to create a fake $20 bill as it took for him to paint one of the paintings. If he had chosen to sell his paintings, he could have been a successful artist. Sadly, after he left prison he was never heard from again.

Thoughts: When we work solely for profit as the end goal our efforts can become misdirected. To gain true wealth one must work with the end product in mind and not the profit to be gained. Then the money will follow. We all work to put food on the table, but it is more spiritually rewarding to work for a cause that is morally sound. It is better to work as a gardener knowing that you are helping to make your neighborhood more beautiful than to earn more money in a position that is unethical.

Source: This is a true story. I first heard this tale on a CD of inspirational speeches by Zig Ziglar.

Classroom Ideas: Challenge the students to make a painting illustrating a mistake they have made in the past. Then turn the tables by asking them to depict the outcome they would now choose.

****

"Success is...
to laugh often and much,
to appreciate beauty,
to find the best in others,
to leave the world a bit better,
to know even one life has breathed easier
because you have lived."
-Emerson

****

"Red Sails" Painting by Hirschten

MA LIANG AND THE MAGIC PAINTBRUSH

Audience: All Ages

Once upon a time there was a poor boy named Ma Liang. One night he dreamed that a wise man gifted him a magic paintbrush. When he awoke he found a paintbrush like the one from his dream in his desk. Using this new brush he painted the image of a cricket onto a sheet of paper. The moment Ma Liang finished the painting it came to life. The cricket then jumped off of the table. Ma Liang used the magic brush to help his neighbors get the things they needed to make life easier.

A greedy man noticed Ma Liang's use of the magic paintbrush. He wanted to steal it to make treasures for himself. The greedy man waited until Ma Liang was walking along the road without his friends. The man grabbed Ma Liang and the paintbrush. Ma Liang was thrown into the dungeon of the greedy man's house.

The man immediately tried to draw a chest full of treasures on the wall but the image did not come to life. Realizing that the magic brush must not work without Ma Liang, the boy was dragged from the dungeon and asked to draw a mountain of gold. Clever Ma Liang drew a mountain of gold on an island in the middle of the ocean. A boat was added to the scene. The greedy man jumped onto the boat sailing quickly toward the mountain. Ma Liang then drew many rivers and valleys between them. He placed dragons to guard the land from the greedy man on the shore of the ocean. For his selfishness he was banished from his homeland.

Ma Liang went on painting things of beauty to share with his good neighbors and lived happily ever after.

Thoughts: If you create art for a greedy reason the work will fall flat. It won't have the spark of "life" that is so appealing in work that is created in the spirit of giving.

Source: This is a Chinese folktale.

Classroom Ideas: Prompt children by asking what they would draw to help their neighbors. If you want dramatic artwork ask them to illustrate how they would trick the greedy man. (This can bring out a lot of feelings of revenge, however, so watch out!)

Prompt adults by asking them in what ways they could use their artwork to help others.

****

"There are some people who live in a dream world, and there are some that face reality; and then there are those that turn one into the other."
-Douglas H. Everett

****

"Blooms at Each of My Steps" Painting of Isadora Duncan by Hirschten

ISADORA DUNCAN, FOUNDER OF MODERN DANCE

Audience: Age 8 and up

Isadora Duncan started dancing at a very young age. At age 6 she offered dance classes to her fellow neighborhood children for pocket change. She continued learning and teaching. When she became an adult, she moved from

California to New York City. She worked there in professional dance troupes.

Duncan found the restrictive methods of traditional dance to be too oppressive for her tastes. She preferred to dance without the point shoes and corsets that a ballerina had to wear. She wanted for her body to be able to move about naturally. Inspired by the waves in the ocean she wanted her arms to move in fluid motions. Most importantly she preferred to dance improvisationally, without a preset combination of steps.

Moving to London in 1898, Duncan found that the European audiences were more receptive to her style of dance. Gradually she gained a following. In 1902 she started touring the globe, performing in many different countries. She started schools of dance, teaching many students her influential new style.

Tragedy struck in 1913 when both of her children drowned in a car accident. This event tainted the rest of her life. In 1927, at the age of fifty, she also died in an accident when her long scarf got caught in the wheel of a car.

While Isadora Duncan's story ended sadly, her influence on the development of dance was profound. Her rebellious nature paved the way for new techniques and styles. She is considered to be the founder of modern dance.

Thoughts: The most important take away from Duncan's story is how she was able to break the traditional trends to develop something new. She didn't like the ballet shoes so she took them off.

Source: This is a true story. Read Isadora Duncan's autobiography, "*My Life*."

Classroom Ideas: Encourage your students to 'think outside the box.' In art class this may mean questioning whether we should paint with a brush, splatter paint or use our fingers. Whenever students think of an innovative way of solving an artistic problem, encourage them. They may start a new innovative trend.

****

"Now I am going to reveal to you something which is very pure, a totally white thought, it blooms at each of my steps...
The dance is love, it is only love, it alone, and that is enough. I would like to no longer dance to anything but the rhythm of my soul."
-Isadora Duncan

****

"The Fall of Icarus" Illustration by Hirschten

THE FALL OF ICARUS

Audience: Age 8 and up

Once upon a time there was an artist named Daedalus. He could create every form of art imaginable. He could paint. He could sculpt. He even designed grand buildings.

One day the king asked Daedalus to make a complicated maze called a labyrinth. It was designed so that when a person went into it, he could not find the way out. A monstrous creature that was half man and half bull, a Minotaur, was placed at the center of the maze. The king would put his enemies into the labyrinth where they would be eaten by the Minotaur.

The king's daughter, the princess, fell in love with a man named Theseus. The king hated him. Fearing that his daughter would marry this enemy, the king had Theseus thrown into the labyrinth. The princess went to the artist Daedalus and begged him to tell her the secret of the maze so that she could save Theseus. Daedalus explained that she could tie a string to a tree outside the maze and pull it in with her. She could then find her lover and follow the string back out.

The princess followed Daedalus' advice and escaped with Theseus. They fled to a faraway land and were married.

When the king found out what his daughter had done, he knew that the artist had given her the secret of the maze. In his anger he banished Daedalus to an island prison.

Daedalus and his son, Icarus, were forced to live at the top of a prison tower. Below the tower soldiers marched, guarding them.

Daedalus created a plan of escape from the prison. They could not get a boat to sail away because the soldiers would see them. Daedalus planned to make wings so that they could fly over the heads of the soldiers and away to safety.

For years Daedalus collected feathers from birds that flew around the tower. When he had gathered enough, he glued the feathers to his son's arms and then to his own. Daedalus warned Icarus that when they flew off they must stay above the water so that the wings did not get wet. They must also avoid flying near the sun. The sun could melt the glue and the wings would fall off. Finally, they were ready. Daedalus and Icarus lifted off of the tower and flew through the air.

Daedalus stayed at a steady course between the water and the sun. But Icarus got very excited. He swooped down to the water and back up again above his father. Down and up, up and down he went until he went as high as the wind would take him. The sun melted the glue off of his wings. Feathers fell from his arms. Icarus dropped into the water and drowned. The artist, Daedalus, reached the mainland and escaped to freedom. Yet he was saddened by the loss of his son. Although he gained his freedom, he lost his most valued treasure.

Thoughts: Creation is a powerful tool. Just like the

ability to fly in this story, our ability to create new things must be harnessed if it is to help us reach our goals. We can soar up and down but if our eyes aren't on the prize we can veer off track and lose sight of our destination. It could be said that creating the beautiful wings was Daedalus' goal, but maybe the goal was beyond that artform. The goal of reaching land eluded Icarus. Having said that there is always room for redemption according to the writer of this story, Ovid. The character Icarus falls to his death yet Ovid was adamant that there is "no death, but only change and innovation." His writing assures us that we should not fear mistakes. No matter what the outcome is, "the only constant is change."

Source: This is a Greek myth that was written down by the poet, Ovid, in his "*Metamorphosis*."

Classroom Ideas: Matisse did a wonderful cut paper collage depicting the fall of Icarus. Pair this story with a study on Matisse and collage. Ask the students to collage images to illustrate this story or other Greek myths.

****

"As wave is driven by wave
And each , pursued, pursues the wave
ahead,
So time flies on and follows, flies, and
follows,
Always, forever and new.
What was before is left behind;
What never was is now;
And every passing moment is renewed.
Be assured, there is no death-
No death,
But only change and innovation.
The sum of all things remains the same."
-Ovid

****

"The Story of Shakuntala" Illustration by Hirschten

KOLAM

Audience: All Ages

In the state of Tamil Nadu in the southernmost part of India, the women perform a special ritual every morning. Before sunrise they go to the front of their homes, clean the ground or pavement and then create a drawing called a Kolam.

The Kolam is a form of Rangoli design made with either rice or chalk powder. These powders are dyed with a wide variety of colors. To start the Kolam, the women measure

207

out a symmetrical pattern with dots. Then they challenge themselves to fill in the pattern with one continuous line. This represents the unity of all life on the planet. Sometimes images of animals such as fish and birds are incorporated into the designs.

Kolams can be used as a sign to welcome others into a home. Sometimes they are used to decorate for a holiday or wedding celebration. Other times they are used to honor specific Hindu Gods or Goddesses.

Patterns used to create the Kolams are often passed down from family members, one generation to the next. This morning, the women in Tamil Nadu created Kolam designs in front of their homes. Tomorrow, they will do it again.

Thoughts: Just as the natural world renews itself each day, the artists who create the Kolam designs renew their patterns each morning. Art can be used as a meditative practice to remember and honor the sacred patterns of nature. To create a piece of art that will be destroyed is also a lesson in nonattachment.

Source: This is a true story. Read "*Rangoli: An Indian Art Activity Book*" by Suma O'Farrell for step-by-step patterns for children.

Classroom Ideas: Study traditional Kolam designs, then create them on the front steps to your school. Another similar option is to study Tibetan Sand Mandalas. These designs are also destroyed after they are completed. For those provide the students with round cardboard pieces to create their design on. After they are finished they must be swept away.

****

"A gift is pure when it is given from the heart and when we expect nothing in return."
-Ved Vyasa, The Bhagavad Gita

****

"Self-portrait" Painting by Vincent Van Gogh

VAN GOGH

Audience: Teens and up

Vincent Van Gogh was born in the Netherlands in 1853. His father was a church minister. He considered going into that profession but ended up working as an art dealer when he reached adulthood. Van Gogh was a successful art dealer for a few years in London and Paris until he lost his job. He decided to study art after attempting to go to ministerial school.

211

Van Gogh made many, many paintings and drawings over the course of his career. He had a distinctive style that used bold lines and brushwork to create definition and texture. He loved painting the countryside and the patterns found in nature.

Sadly, Van Gogh was not as successful at selling his own paintings as he had been selling other artist's work when he was a dealer. The last years of his life were spent in the south of France. He painted the bright colors found in the warmer climate there.

Very few people were interested in Van Gogh's work with the exception of his brother, Theo. Vincent and Theo wrote many letters to each other. In them Van Gogh wrote a lot about why he loved to paint.

One reason Van Gogh struggled to gain credibility as an artist during his lifetime was because he suffered from mental illness. Evidence of this instability occurred when he cut off part of his ear. He was distressed that his fellow artist friend, Gauguin, was leaving town. Later Van Gogh committed suicide: ending his life at the age of only thirty-seven.

After his death, Vincent Van Gogh's works gained popularity. They are now considered to be the masterworks of the Post-Impressionist era.

Thoughts: It is difficult for us to know how much of Van Gogh's anguish was the result of his mental illness or lack of support from the art community. His work was innovative for the time so most people dismissed its value. Everyone who is an artist needs encouragement so that their voice will develop with strength. Remember this before you dismiss innovative art. Everyone's voice has value.

Source: This is a true story. There are numerous books that document Vincent's letters to his brother, Theo.

Classroom Ideas: Pair this story with a study of the post-impressionist movement. Many teachers use Van Gogh's "Bedroom in Arles" painting as a perfect example of the use of perspective. Another idea is to study Van Gogh's many self-portraits, then have the students create ones of themselves.

****

"Love many things, for therein lies the true strength, and whosoever loves much performs much, and can accomplish much, and what is done in love is done well."
-Vincent Van Gogh

****

"Transformation" Illustration by Hirschten

FEAST OF STONE SOUP

Audience: All Ages

Once upon a time there were three soldiers who were returning home after a horrible war. The soldiers had to walk for days. They were tired and had run out of food.

They came to a village. Hoping for a meal, they knocked on the door of a house. When someone came to the door, the soldiers asked for food but were told that there wasn't enough in the house to share. They knocked on the next door, but again were told that there wasn't enough to feed them.

The soldiers went to the square in the center of town. One of them began picking up stones off the ground. A curious little boy asked, "What are you doing with those stones?" "Well, I am going to make stone soup," said the soldier. "But I need a big pot to boil it in. Do you have such a pot?" "We do," said the boy. "I'll go get it."

When the boy returned they placed the pot on the ground over a fire pit. They brought water from the well to fill the pot. The soldiers dropped the stones in it.

By this time a crowd of people had gathered to watch the making of the stone soup. One of the soldiers took out a spoon and tasted the water. "Hmmm," he said. "It needs something." People in the crowd piped in, "I have carrots we could add." "I have potatoes." "I have rosemary." The soldier smiled, "Well, bring them please!"

The villagers brought the food and added it to the water until the soup was thick. The smell of it wafted through the air of the village. "Let's bring out tables," suggested one person. Tables were brought to the square. Fabrics were draped over the tables. Flowers were gathered from the fields and put in vases for decoration. Children drew colorful pictures on the sidewalks with chalk.

Finally the townspeople sat down to share the soup with the soldiers. Everyone was amazed that such a feast could be made from just a few stones.

Thoughts: Far more can be accomplished when people work together on a common task. Then everyone gains. Holding in your resources often creates isolation.

Source: This is a folktale found in several different European countries. My favorite rendition is by Marcia Brown. Written in 1947, Brown's "*Stone Soup*" won the Caldecott Metal.

Classroom Ideas: This story is best matched with a collaborative project. There are many options but one of my favorites is to purchase multiple canvas boards. Lay them on the floor and draw out a Celtic knot design over all of them. Distribute the boards to the students, asking them to paint whatever they want within the designs drawn. When you are finished put them together as a large collaborative work.

****

"Where there is hatred, let me sow love.
It is in loving that we are loved.
It is in giving that we receive.
It is in pardoning that we are pardoned."
-Saint Francis of Assisi

****

PART 8

FINDING THE MUSE

"The Muses" Illustration by Hirschten

THE MUSES

Audience: All Ages

In the land of ancient Greece, there was a natural spring where water bubbled up out of the ground. The winged horse named Pegasus flew down to this spring. As he drank the water his hooves gently touched the ground. From his footsteps nine beautiful women were born.

These women became known as the Muses. Each of them had a special talent. For example, one was a poet, one was a musician and one was a dancer. When they created their art, new ideas would come to humans. These inspirations began guiding artists all around the world. Zeus, king of the Gods, gathered the Muses to his side. They lived in the heavens of Mount Olympus.

One day a horrible creature called the Sphinx was inspired by the Muses to write a riddle. The Sphinx had the head of a woman and the body of a winged lion. She had a taste for humans. She began pouncing on people who entered into the forest. Each person she attacked was asked the riddle. If they answered incorrectly she would eat them.

The riddle seemed impossible to solve. Everyone who encountered the Sphinx was killed. Soon the people of the land proclaimed that anyone who defeated the Sphinx would be rewarded handsomely. A clever man named Oedipus decided to face this challenge. He prayed to the Muses to guide him to the correct answer.

Oedipus entered the forest alone. He walked for miles on a twisty dirt path until the Sphinx jumped out from the bushes, knocking him down. She asked him the riddle. "What animal is born four footed, becomes two footed, become three footed and then four footed again?" The Sphinx licked her lips as she laughed. The claws on her paws scratched Oedipus.

The answer came to him. "It is a human," he said, "for when we are babies we crawl on all fours. When we are grown up we walk on two legs. As we age we use a cane to help us walk, which gives us three legs. Then when we become very old we return to all fours, unable to stand."

The Sphinx roared in shock. Oedipus seized his chance. Lifting his sword, he killed the beast.

The people of Thebes made Oedipus their king for defeating the monster. Oedipus received his reward and was forever grateful to the Muses for guiding him to the correct answer.

Throughout time, the Muses continue to give gifts of artistic talent to mortal humans.

Thoughts: The sources of inspiration can be as varied and diverse as the nine Muses. Whatever your source is, let it guide you to defeat the monsters. Let it guide you to solve problems.

Source: This is a story derived from Greek mythology.

The story of the Muses was documented in Hesiod's "*Theogony*."

Classroom Ideas: Children are especially drawn to the Sphinx monster both for her form and her riddles. Illustrate this story and have a moment for sharing favorite riddles. Also riddles can be a good entry level reading for beginning readers. Asking first or second graders to read riddles aloud can be excellent practice.

Adults are fascinated with the idea of the Muse. Ask them what the source of their inspiration is. You will be surprised at the wide variety of answers.

****

"Nothing can be created out of nothing."
-Lucretius

****

"Gismonda" Poster by Mucha

MUCHA AND BERNHARDT

Audience: All Ages

On December 26, 1894, Alfons Mucha was working in a print shop correcting proofs in Paris, France. The famous actress Sarah Bernhardt came in and ordered a new poster design to be created for her upcoming theater show, "Gismonda." Mucha had never created an advertising poster design before but he was the only artist available to take the job. Bernhardt needed the job done in just a few days, so Mucha took on the project despite the short notice and holiday festivities. Using Bernhardt's beauty as his inspiration he created a dynamic design.

Soon Mucha's muse, Bernhardt, became his salvation. When the poster was printed, Mucha's boss did not care for the design. He gave it to Bernhardt anyway, however, because she had wanted the job done quickly. When the actress received the package, she sent for Mucha to come visit her apartment immediately. As he arrived, Bernhardt embraced him. She told him, "You have made me immortal." She loved the poster and asked Mucha to sign a six year contract to produce more posters as well as dress designs.

Mucha became a Parisian celebrity overnight when the new poster hit the streets on January 1st, 1895. He continued to work successfully as an illustrator and painter until his death in the 1930s.

Thoughts: What is most striking about this story is how Mucha's boss did not care for his first poster design. What if he had refused to give the poster to Bernhardt? Mucha's success relied on the favor of just a couple of individuals who could not have foreseen the subsequent enormous popularity of his art. Art is about innovation. We have to wonder how many other artists in the course of history who created innovative works were shot down by old-fashioned business owners. All too often art is selected for promotion because of preconceived notions of what will sell as opposed to what the public is actually hungry for.

Source: This is a true story. Read the book, *"Mucha,"* by Sarah Mucha.

Classroom Ideas: Share this story and ask your students to design a poster for a theater show, band, or favorite group.

****

*"Art is the child of nature in whom we trace
the features of the mother's face."
- Henry Wadsworth Longfellow*

****

"The Work of the Soul" Painting by Hirschten

1,000 PAPER CRANES

Audience: Age 8 and up

According to an ancient Japanese legend, anyone who folds 1,000 paper cranes will be granted one wish. The paper cranes are made using origami paper folding techniques. They can be made in a wide variety of colors. Often the paper cranes are strung together and hung like garlands.

When Sadako Susaki turned twelve, she heard this legend from her best friend Chizuko Hamamoto. She decided to try to fold 1,000 paper cranes herself so that she could be granted a wish. She would wish for good health. Sadako was suffering from leukemia, a type of cancer. When she was two years old the United States, in war with Japan, dropped an atomic bomb on her home, the city of Hiroshima. The bomb exposed her to harmful radiation that made her very ill. Sadako started to fold paper cranes but only managed to complete 644 of them. She died on October 25, 1955. Sadako's friends and family completed the 1,000 paper crane project in her honor.

A statue of Sadako holding a golden crane now stands in the Hiroshima Peace Memorial Park in Japan. On it is written the inscription, "This is our cry. This is our prayer. Peace in the world." Every year on the anniversary of the dropping of the atomic bomb, August 6th, the people of Hiroshima celebrate "Peace Day." On this day many people shroud the statue of Sadako with paper cranes.

Thoughts: Behind this sad tale is a lesson to be learned about the horrors of war. When people fold paper cranes today in honor of Sadako, they are reminding us of this story in the hopes that we will not repeat this mistake again. This is a perfect example of how art can be used as a powerful, yet gentle, tool to push for political change.

Source: This is a true story. An excellent chapter book retelling this story was written in 1977 by Eleanor Coerr entitled "*Sadako and the Thousand Paper Cranes.*"

Classroom Ideas: Learn the art of origami together. Be sure to have clear handouts to illustrate the steps for your students. I find describing the steps difficult to explain!

****

"Unfolding its freight
Spilling new rainwater,
The camellia bends. "
-Matsuo Basho

****

"Impression III" Painting by Kandinsky Circa 1911

KANDINSKY'S ART

Audience: All Ages

Wassily Kandinsky was a Russian artist who was born in Moscow in 1866. In the first part of his life he studied law and economics. At age 30, however, he gave up his successful teaching career to study painting. He loved the French impressionists and was drawn to bright vivid colors. He settled in Germany in 1896 where he found people to be more open to his modern theories of art than in Russia.

In the beginning, Kandinsky painted landscapes. But with time, he focused more on painting his inner spiritual world than the outer world. Using fewer and fewer recognizable symbols, Kandinsky was one of the first artists to create abstract paintings. When he painted, he wanted to express the emotions of his soul. Kandinsky wrote about his ideas in his famous book *"Concerning the Spiritual in Art."* In it he stated, "That is beautiful which is produced by the inner need, which springs from the soul." He wanted for color to reflect a harmonious chord with the soul. He often listened to music to find inspiration for his paintings.

Between 1922 and 1933, Kandinsky taught art at the famous Bauhaus Schools in Germany until they were closed by the Nazis. As Kandinsky and many of his fellow artists fled to France, the Nazi party seized several of his paintings and exhibited them in a show called "Degenerate Art." The purpose of this show was to make fun of modern art like Kandinsky's. After the show the artwork that had been on display was destroyed. This did not deter Kandinsky, however. He spent the last years of his life creating dynamic paintings that were inspired by geometry.

Thoughts: Inspiration for artwork can be found outside of ourselves and within. If you are confused about the meaning behind modern art, ask the artist what inspired him or her. The source may surprise you.

Source: This is a true story. Read Kandinsky's book, *"Concerning the Spiritual in Art."*

Classroom Ideas: One of my favorite exercises to do with students is to study Kandinsky's art and then create abstract paintings inspired by music. First ask the students to listen to music without painting. After a minute, stop the music. Ask them to select the colors they feel are reflected in the music. Turn the music back on and have them start their painting. Sometimes I will even ask the students to close their eyes for the first minute of painting. This helps them to focus on the rhythm of the music and not worry about the final outcome of the painting.

****

"The aim of art is not to reproduce the outward appearance of things but their inner significance."
-Aristotle

****

"Inspired by Frida Khalo's Journal" Illustration by Hirschten

FRIDA KHALO

Audience: Age 8 and up

Frida Kahlo was born in what is now Mexico City in 1907. She thought she wanted to study medicine but became engrossed in art after she was in a traffic accident as a teenager.

While riding a bus in 1925, Kahlo was injured when the vehicle collided with a trolley car. A metal pole pierced her stomach. Her back, collarbone and pelvis were broken.

After the accident, she was put into a full body cast for three months. Kahlo began painting while recovering from the injuries to pass the time and to express everything she was thinking and feeling. Her mother had a special painting easel made so that she could work while lying down in bed. Many of her paintings were self-portraits filled with symbolic images within her body.

A few years after the accident, Kahlo took four of her paintings to an artist she admired named Diego Rivera. She asked him for his opinion of her work and for his advice. Rivera praised Kahlo's work and encouraged her to continue painting. The two artists fell in love and were married in 1929. Their relationship had many ups and downs. Kahlo was especially saddened when she had several stillborn children.

Kahlo never fully recovered from the accident. She suffered chronic pain because of it throughout her life. She was able to walk again for many years until her right leg became infected with gangrene and had to be amputated. Shortly after this surgery she died of poor health at the age of 47.

Thoughts: Most of us will not suffer the horrific health problems Kahlo experienced after her accident. We all, however, experience the ups and downs of life. Art can be used as a way of expressing how we feel about our experiences. Art can be therapeutic, especially in times of tragedy and healing.

Source: This is a true story. Read *"The Diary of Frida Kahlo: An Intimate Self-Portrait"* for a glimpse into Kahlo's personal diary.

Classroom Ideas: Ask your students to create self-portraits inspired by Frida Kahlo's work. Encourage them to incorporate symbols and distortions to their form in order to express what they are feeling.

****

"My painting contains in it the message of pain. It is not revolutionary. Painting completed my life. I lost three children and a series of other things that would have fulfilled my life. My painting took the place of all of this."
-Frida Kahlo

****

THE AMERICAN FLAG

Audience: All Ages

In 1958, Robert Heft was 17 years old and attending high school in Lancaster, Ohio. Everyone was talking about how the territories of Alaska and Hawaii might soon become states. Heft decided to create a new design of the American flag, adding the two new stars. When he submitted the design to his teacher for a class project, he was given a grade of B-. The teacher jokingly said that if his design was accepted as the new flag the grade would be raised to an A.

Heft sent his flag design to the current president of the United States, Dwight D. Eisenhower. When Alaska and

Hawaii became states later that year, Eisenhower had to choose a new design. Out of the 1,500 designs sent to the president, Heft's flag was chosen!

Heft's teacher kept the promise and raised his grade to an A. As an adult, Robert Heft later became a high school teacher, professor, and mayor of Napoleon, Ohio.

Thoughts: Everyone has different opinions, especially on the subject of art. One person, like Heft's teacher, might dislike a design while another might love it. We should never give too much credibility to one person who likes or dislikes a piece of art. "One man's junk is another man's treasure."

Source: This is a true story. Listen to a recording of Robert Heft sharing his story on the StoryCorps website.

Classroom Ideas: Flag design has a long and creative history. Create a flag design for your school, family, state, or country. Flags created by pirates like Blackbeard are especially rich with symbolism.

****

"Make visible what, without you,
might never have been seen. "
-Robert Bresson

****

"Cellular Structure" Painting by Hirschten

RORSCHACH AND THE INKBLOT TESTS

Audience: All Ages

In Europe in the late 1800s, a card game called "Blotto" became popular. The game consisted of premade cards that had blots of ink splattered on them. The players would look at these blots, searching for images. They would then write poems inspired by what they saw and share them with their fellow players.

The Swiss psychologist, Hermann Rorschach, used the ideas from the game "Blotto" to develop his tests for mental health. He created inkblot pictures and then asked his patients to describe what images they saw. Rorschach believed that what the patients saw told a lot about their personality. This test was also used to encourage the patients to discuss memories from their past, their desires and their fears. This way, the psychologist could help the patient work through personal problems.

Many artists have used inkblots to inspire their paintings. These artists include Leonardo da Vinci, Botticelli, Victor Hugo, Salvador Dali, and Andy Warhol.

Thoughts: No two people will interpret images in the exact same way because of their individuality and personal experiences. If a viewer sees an image in an abstract painting, such as an inkblot, this reveals the personality of the viewer. It does not necessarily reflect the intent of the artist.

Source: This is a true story. Read the excellent children's book, "*Inkblot; Drip, Splat and Squish Your Way to Creativity*," by Margaret Peot for more ideas on creating your own inkblot art.

Classroom Ideas: Have students create inkblot art using ink drippers and absorbent paper. Have them title the work according to what images they see or write poetry inspired by the images like the original "Blotto" game.

****

"Art does not reproduce what we see rather
it makes us see."
-Paul Klee

****

"The Secret Garden" Painting by Hirschten

THE SECRET GARDEN

Audience: All Ages

Once upon a time a little Scottish girl named Jane went to a party. As the grownups talked, she wandered throughout the house looking at the pictures on the walls and the interesting knick-knacks on the shelves. Then she saw a glass door leading out to a garden. She opened it, stepping into a lush green space. Flowers speckled the ground. A delicate tree arched its branches over her as if it were hugging the garden. Nestled into the earth of a hill, someone had placed a large shell, the largest shell Jane had ever seen. She was able to hide under the lip of the shell, then peer out onto the quiet of the garden. Jane imagined fairies dancing around her. Brick walls enclosed the yard making it a true secret garden.

When she went back to the party, Jane told her hostess how she had found the garden. They both agreed that it was a magical space.

Years later, Jane returned to Scotland as an adult and went by the old house hoping to see the secret garden again. Sadly, she found that the yard had been paved over. It was now a parking lot. The plants, trees, flowers, and even the shell were gone.

Thoughts: As the designers of our space, our world, we have the power of choice. With our hands we can create a secret garden or a parking lot. If you don't like what you see you have the power to transform it. I love envisioning the parking lot being transformed back into a beautiful secret garden. This may seem like a sad story to end this book with, but I don't believe it has to be. You can transform our world with the power of your creative energy. My challenge to you is to gain the courage to do it.

Source: This is a personal account shared with me by my fourth grade teacher, Mrs. Jane Luhn.

Classroom Ideas: Have students brainstorm what they would like to see in a space that is now a parking lot. Design plans and discuss the endless possibilities. You can also read the classic book, *"The Secret Garden,"* by Frances Hodgson Burnett.

****

"Learn to cultivate your own garden."
-Voltaire

****

CONCLUSION

"The Birds of Syria" Painting by Hirschten

TOP TEN REASONS TO CREATE ART

The reasons we create art are as diverse as the many artists of
the world. Sometimes artists conflict because they do not
understand that the motivation for another artist may be
different from their own. Through art we can come to better

understand ourselves and each other. Art is unique to the human experience. If we truly value diversity and the worth of every person we must strive to understand the various reasons for creating art.

I found that these stories, gathered from a wide variety of cultures, help to articulate the purpose of art. After compiling them, I created this list of the top ten reasons I see for being an artist. Can you and your students think of any others?

1. **To Communicate Our Values** Art can convey a message to the viewer. Political art clearly goes into this category. We often want to share our experiences whether it is in celebration or anger. Art can be used to help others understand what it is to be another person with different values, skin tone, or culture. When a truth is expressed, people listen. *Art is a language that expresses what we often can't say with words.* Art that communicates values is a powerful tool that can transform cultures. If you create landscape art because you value the environment you are communicating your values. We often create more of what we want to see in the world.

2. **To Build Community** Art is often a solitary endeavor that builds relationships between the artist and the viewer only after the product is finished. It can, however, be used to bring teams of people together as they create a group project.

3. **To Challenge Ourselves** Sometimes we need direction. Focusing our energy on accurately depicting a mountain stream can help an artist find direction in life. Pushing ourselves to the limit of our abilities is healthy and promotes innovation.

4. **To Open Our Eyes** When we look at a flower for hours on end in order to recreate it in artistic form, we view it in a whole new way. We break it apart, dissecting it until every detail is more apparent to us. Art can open our eyes to the miraculous patterns found in nature. We observe our world and appreciate it more fully. Henry Miller said it best when he wrote, "The moment one gives close attention to anything, even a blade of grass, it becomes a mysterious, awesome, indescribably magnificent world in itself."

5. **To Honor the Sacred** Many artists share their reverence for the divine through art. Art can be used to express

religious devotion. It can also be used to honor the sacred beauty of the natural world.

6. **To Create More Beauty in the World** William Morris, founder of the Arts and Crafts Movement, wrote, "Have nothing in your house that you do not believe to be useful and believe to be beautiful." He believed that we should not fill our lives with ugly things. Artists who fit this category create art with the purpose of filling our homes and communities with more beauty. The Aesthetic Movement and the writings of Oscar Wilde may interest artists with this purpose. (Now for extra credit points: define beauty! Ha ha.)

7. **To Articulate Our Purpose** Art can be used to narrow down our goals. It can help us to articulate what it is we want to say before we make our final exit. Sometimes I will have students who think that they will use painting to express their message but soon find that writing or another art form would suit their needs better.

8. **To Heal Ourselves** If you are angry, happy, sad or in love you can use art to express your emotions. The purpose of this art form is to heal the artist by letting out pent up feelings, not to create a product. If this appeals to you, you

may be interested in Art Therapy. This form of art has its roots in the German Expressionist Movement, a group of artists who used art to reflect their internal world and were influenced by Freud, Jung and other psychologists.

9. **To Understand the Human Experience** When we create art, it can show us a lot about ourselves. When we examine the work of others, it can help us to understand other people's experiences. We are more alike than our differences. It can show what people are afraid of, what they value, what they love, what they are attracted to. Art reflects the experiences of the people who create it. When seeing the work of others, we can see ourselves reflected in that mirror and gain a better understanding of what unites the human experience.

10. **To Enjoy Ourselves** Sometimes it is as simple as that. We create art for the enjoyment of creating art. When we do this, we are participating in the great cosmic dance, being active, being alive. Many art movements have campaigned for this purpose. The Decadent Movement proclaimed "L'Art pour L'Art [Art for Art's Sake]." After Zen Buddhist writings such as "*Zen and the Art of Archery*" were published in the west artists strived to enjoy the process of art more than

the product. The Process Art Movement and Jackson Pollack fell into this category.

In conclusion...

The reason a person creates art can influence their style but it doesn't have to. Another element to respecting each other is recognizing that when a style is different from our own it does not mean the art is "bad" or "not art." There is room for a diverse range of styles in the art world. Just as "one man's junk is another man's treasure," recognize that even if a work of art doesn't speak to you it might be important to someone else.

I firmly believe that anyone can be an artist if that is what they desire to be. To hone your craft can take time and determination but the rewards of the experience are worth it.

May these reasons to create art inspire you to find your voice. I want to hear what you have to say.

SUGGESTED READING FOR CHILDREN

These are picture books that I recommend for the elementary art classroom.

Alborozo, Gabriel. *Let's Paint*. Allen & Unwin, 2014.

Alts, Marta. *I Am An Artist*. MacMillian Children's Books, 2013.

Brumbeau, Jeff. *The Quiltmaker's Gift*. Orchard Books, 2000.

dePaola, Tomie. *The Art Lesson*. Turtleback Books, 1997.

Emberly, Ed. *Go Away Big Green Monster*. Little Brown and Co., 1992.

Flournoy, Valerie. *The Patchwork Quilt*. FBAPowersetup, 1995.

Johnson, Crockett. *Harold and the Purple Crayon*. HarperCollins, 2005.

Kennedy, Richard. *The Porcelain Man*. Little, Brown and Company, 1976.

Leo, Lionni. *Matthew's Dream*. Knopf, 1995.

Massenot, Veronique. *The Three Musicians*. Prestel, 2013.

McPhail, David. *Drawing Lessons from a Bear*. Little, Brown Books, 2000.

Meinderts, Koos. *The Man in the Clouds*. Lemniscaat, 2012.

Pinkwater, Daniel. *Bear's Picture*. HMH Books for Young Readers, 2008.

Pinkwater, D. Manus. *The Big Orange Splot*. Scholastic Paperbacks, 1993.

Pirotta, Saviour. *Patrick Paints a Picture*. Frances Lincoln Children's Books, 2007.

Pomerantz, Charlotte. *The Chalk Dolls*. HarperCollins, 1993.

Portis, Antionette. *Not a Box*. HarperCollins, 2006.

Reynolds, Peter. *Sky Color*. Candlewick Press, 2012.

Taback, Simms. *Joseph had a Little Overcoat*. Penguin Group, 2000.

Ziefert, Harriet. *Lunchtime for Purple Snake*. HMH Books for Young Readers, 2008.

SUGGESTED READING FOR ADULTS

Cameron, Julia. *The Artist's Way.* Jeremy P. Tarcher/Putnam, 2002.

Frankl, Viktor E. *Man's Search for Meaning.* Beacon Press, 2006.

Godin, Seth. *The Icarus Deception.* Portfolio Hardcover, 2012.

Holt, David and Bill Mooney. *Ready-to-Tell Tales.* August House, 1994.

Kandinsky, Wassily. *Concerning the Spiritual in Art.* Dover Publications; Reprint, 1977.

Kent, Corita. *Learning by Heart: Teachings to Free the Creative Spirit.* Allworth Press, 2008.

Lamott, Anne. *Bird by Bird: Some Instructions on Writing and Life.* Anchor, 1995.

Lee, Jennifer. *The Right-Brain Business Plan: A Creative, Visual Map for Success.* New World Library, 2011.

Lipman, Doug. *Improving Your Storytelling: Beyond the Basics for All Who Tell Stories in Work and Play.*

August House, 1999.

Livo, Norma J. *Bring Out Their Best: Values Education and Character Development through Traditional Tales.* Libraries Unlimited, 2003.

O'Donohue, John. *Beauty: The Invisible Embrace.* Harper Perennial. 2005.

Pearmain, Elisa Davy. *Doorways to the Soul: 52 Wisdom Tales from Around the World.* Resource Publications, 1998.

Shelley, Mary. *Frankenstein.* Dover Publications; Reprint, 1994.

Tesdell, Diana. *Stories of Art and Artists.* Everyman's Library, 2014.

Wilde, Oscar. *The Picture of Dorian Gray.* Dover Publications; Reprint, 1993.

Hirschten dressed as an "artist" at age 9
(Her idea of what an artist is has changed since then! Moustaches are not required.)

ABOUT THE AUTHOR

Artist Addie Hirschten is a contemporary impressionist painter, author and public speaker. She teaches painting with the Indianapolis Art Center and hosts the podcast "The Alchemy of Art."

Hirschten earned a Bachelor of Fine Arts from Appalachian State University graduating in the year 2000. After working for a number of years as a children's librarian, she went on to earn a Master of Library Science at Indiana University. When Hirschten moved to Indianapolis, Indiana in 2011, she began conducting performances for children with her company, Fantastic Fables, as well as presenting sermons for Unitarian Universalist churches. During the same time period she started painting daily and posting new paintings on her prolific blog. Hirschten often speaks at schools, churches, libraries and graduations. Her uplifting talks incorporate storytelling and appeal to all age groups.

Find out more at: www.azhirfineart.com

Made in the USA
Middletown, DE
18 August 2015